"An affectionate and very funny look at our nation's diversity… With refreshing honesty, [Kilpatrick] takes the piss out of the lot of us"
– David Bullard, NewsTime

"Required reading for all South Africans… Magnanimous and heart-warming, this book turns out to be a celebration of all the people of South Africa, rather than a critique"

– ZA Difference

"[A] cheeky, comical, daring and delicious read that forces readers not just to accept other races' weird and wacky cultures, but also their own. And by the last page, while drying the tears of laughter from your face, you realise: we may all be crazy but at least we're all South African"
– Rapport

"It's funny because it's true and that's why we love being South African… A brilliant and light-hearted means with which to dissect our layered and wonderful population"

– JHB Live

"This politically irreverent handbook highlights South Africans' quirks, habits and 'cultures'… readers will delight in seeing how they fare among their fellow demographics. This unofficial endorsement of our beloved people would come in handy for visitors and expatriates returning to our shores"

– Cape Times

"The side-splitting  his precise analysis of our Rain rolling down your cheeks as you vi A must-read"
ws

"Gentle and surprisingly funny, *The Racist's Guide* is unlikely to ruffle feathers of any but the most gratuitously sensitive, and its elegantly old-fashioned brand of wit is suitable for all ages"

– Sunday Times

The *racist's* Guide To The People Of South Africa

Simon Kilpatrick

Published by Two Dogs
an imprint of Burnet Media

•

Burnet Media is the publisher of Two Dogs and Mercury books
info@burnetmedia.co.za
www.burnetmedia.co.za
PO Box 53557, Kenilworth, 7745, South Africa

•

First published 2010, reprinted 2010 and 2011 (four times)
7 9 8 6

•

Managing director: Tim Richman
Cover design and layout: Christoff van Wyk
Interior illustrations: Christine Peterson
Proofreader: Ania Rokita

•

Distributed by Jacana Media www.jacana.co.za

Printed and bound by Ultra Litho, Johannesburg

•

ISBN 9781920137328

About the author

Simon Kilpatrick was born and raised in a small town on the outskirts of Johannesburg. He studied accounting at Stellenbosch University and then worked for some years in corporate business, before packing it all up to pursue his desire to travel and to write.

Acknowledgments

Firstly, I would like to thank everyone who contributed to the creation of the book: to Ray with his incredible sense of humour, who provided buckets of inspiration and ideas. To the entire team at Two Dogs for all their hard work. To my editor and publishing manager, Tim Richman, for taking the time to read my manuscript, for his patience and graciousness, and for making the publishing process such a pleasure. A very special thanks to our artist, Christine, for doing such a wonderful pro bono job on the illustrations. And then a huge thanks to all the friends and colleagues who took the time to provide original thought and invaluable feedback.

On a more personal note, thank you to my entire family for their unwavering support and love, and especially to my parents for the sacrifices they've made so that I could live my dream. To my wonderfully eccentric and beautiful wife, without whom I could not be a writer. And to God, for the opportunity and privilege to enjoy the gift of writing.

Finally, thank you to all the fascinating people of South Africa, who gave me something to write about simply by being themselves.

Simon Kilpatrick
October 2010

CONTENTS

Introduction   **9**

Blacks   **11**

*On colours... On precious stones... On
traditional cuisine... On sociability... On job
satisfaction... On technology... On accents...
On sport... On stress and time management...
On the beach... On getting on with animals... On
communism... On the men... On the women*

Whites   **35**

*On making the rules... On how to be
the boss... On not quite cutting it... On
unknown lawmakers... On being excellent
miners... On bending the rules... On thirst...
On romance... On going on holiday...
On affording themselves some
pleasures... On illness*

Afrikaners   **63**

*On being world champions...On
being professionals... On selling ice
cream... On deliciousness... On having
easy-tanning skin... On fun... On sport...
On naming their children... On the men...
On the women... On women's hobbies*

85   **Indians**
             On coming to South Africa... On
             becoming westernised... On spotting the
             difference... On the theory of sales... On
             proximity to sardines... On cookouts...
             On the women... On the men

103   **Coloureds**
             On who they are... On names... On
             being sensitive about nothing... On kissing and
             making up... On extreme makeovers... On car
             shopping... On the community of clowns...
             On searching for identity... On fishing

121   **Miscellaneous**
             Greeks and Portuguese: *On*
             supermarkets... On spotting the difference...
             Dutch and Germans: *On not being Afrikaners...*
             On saving their money... Chinese: *On saving*
             the rhinos... On the silver lining... On South
             African greetings... Jews: *On being undercover...*
             On requiring no discipline... On blowing
             things out of proportion... On still blowing
             things out of proportion... Expatriates:
             On similarities with Afrikaners...
             On the other option

For my parents, my pecan nut and my family

INTRODUCTION

South Africa, unlike many other countries, sure does have a whole array of different races. That makes it an excellent place for someone like me because I love people-watching. It's actually my favourite hobby. South Africa, to me, is a bit like the Galapagos Islands was to that old dead guy Charles Darwin, who discovered millions of different species of plants and animals there. Sometimes I think of *myself* as a bit of a modern-day observer just like Darwin was, except I observe people, where he observed plants and animals. Oh, and unlike Darwin, I don't go around telling people they have monkeys in their family tree. According to some folk that's just plain rude.

Anyway, people in South Africa are always talking about race, which shows you how much we love the topic. But sometimes I have a hard time keeping track of the behaviour and characteristics of all these races, because there are so many of them and they all behave so differently. At first I thought I might just have a bad memory, but then my friend told me that *he* struggles with the exact same thing. He drives buses for a tour company (he has his commercial driver's licence and everything) and he said he gets tons of tourists asking him the question, "What are the people like in South Africa?" He always tries his very best to give a conclusive answer but it's just too complicated, so he ends up just confusing them. The moment my friend told me that, it hit me: we need a guide to the people of South Africa…

Chapter 1:
BLACKS

On colours...

Blacks in South Africa are not actually black. They're brown. I'm not sure why everyone calls them Blacks, but they do. If we were being picky about the issue we should technically call them Browns, but then no-one would know what we were talking about when we said something like, "Browns sure do love to play soccer." So for simplicity's sake we just call them Blacks.

Now if you want to see a real black Black you have to go to West Africa, to countries like Nigeria and Ghana. The Blacks from those countries are as black as midnight. Obviously there are exceptions; South African Blacks who are as black as midnight do exist, but they are rare. Black Blacks from South Africa are so scarce, in fact, that they have a hard time convincing people they're *not* from Nigeria or Ghana (having people think you're from Nigeria or Ghana is a bad thing). Anyway, other than being brown in colour, Blacks are pretty easy to spot. They almost always have above-average-sized lips and their hair is very curly and black.

Blacks originate from a variety of tribes but I'm not going into all that now. Not only does this book not attempt to document the history of tribal Africans, but in all honesty people who aren't Black don't care what tribe a Black is from. Most people couldn't give two hoots if the Black is a Xhosa or a Zulu, as long as he isn't cheeky and he can do a good job for little pay. But more about that later. All you need to know for now is that there are many tribes but essentially they're all Blacks.

On precious stones…

Before the Whites arrived in South Africa, Blacks lived in huts and collected berries and hunted animals. Then the Whites showed up and chased them away. They chased them away to these places called homelands, which was the land furthest away from the where the Whites wanted to live. However, in recent years the Whites have realised that one of the homelands, being the former Transkei, is actually a splendid place with green rolling hills and jagged cliffs and exquisite beaches. So now the Whites are trying to get the Blacks *out* of the homelands so they can enjoy them too.

The Whites also kept some Blacks close to where they wanted to live because they needed Blacks to work for them. These Blacks had to live in places called townships. Townships are residential areas where Blacks lived because they were not allowed to live too close to Whites. The Whites made this rule too; not the Blacks.

But in 1994 the Blacks got to vote and, among other things, they voted not to be forced to live in homelands and townships any more. Since then Blacks have been free to move around and live wherever they want.

When the Blacks all still lived in the homelands and townships they were all poor, but today Blacks can be categorised into four socioeconomic groups, from poorest to richest:

1. Jobless, poor and starving
2. Gardeners and maids
3. Black Diamonds
4. BEE magnates and politicians

The majority of Blacks are jobless, poor and starving. Most of them live in huts in rural areas, shacks in shanty towns, or together with ten other Blacks in a single-bedroom flat. Most people don't know how they get by on virtually no income, but they do, and it is testament to their resilient will to survive.

Gardeners and maids make up approximately 30 percent of all Blacks, although Whites think they make up 90 percent of them. Pretty much every White has a Black maid and gardener, and some fancy Whites have two of each. For many decades, Whites thought it a privilege of being born White to have a maid and a gardener, but in recent years Blacks have also begun to acquire domestic helpers. This development has confused some Whites. Generally Black women work as maids in the house – cleaning, washing and ironing – while Black men work in the garden – mowing lawns, weeding flowerbeds and pruning trees. It is extremely rare to find a Black man working as a maid in the house because Whites believe Black women are better at cleaning, washing and ironing than their male counterparts. So in short: Black women inside, Black men outside.

Black Diamonds are the emerging Black middle class of South Africa. I think the name Black Diamond is a contradiction in terms, because a diamond is actually a compressed piece of coal that turns into a beautiful precious stone after thousands of years underground. So a Black Diamond is actually just a piece of coal that hasn't turned into a diamond yet – not very flattering if you ask me. If I were part of the emerging Black middle class in South Africa I would ask to be called something else, like Black Gold, because Black Gold is actually another name for crude oil. And at over $70 a barrel, Black Gold is worth much more than a dirty piece of coal. Well whatever, that's the name they've been given and everyone else seems be happy with it.

The Black Diamonds are up-and-coming, educated, flashy, confident and aspirant. They have acquired a taste for green-bottle beer and flashy drinks like Southern Comfort with Appletiser. They drive nice cars and have moved to the previously White-only suburbs. They have wallets brimming with credit cards and they've learnt quickly how to use them. That's why every major corporate company in South Africa is targeting the Black Diamonds with their marketing strategies. You can pretty much sell anything to a Black Diamond – cars, shoes, leather couches, flatscreen TVs, iPods and, really, anything that looks nice.

Becoming a Black Diamond is a fairly lengthy process, but is not actually that complicated:

> Be born Black.

> Get a school education.

> Go to university and get a degree.

> Get a job with a big corporate company and earn a nice salary every month.

> Buy a pair of leather shoes and an expensive suit.

> Buy a black car (silver will do at a push).

> Park your car outside your shack or hut where everyone can see it.

> Buy lots of junk you don't need.

BEE magnates and politicians are the richest Blacks and they've got so stinking rich they don't know what to do with their money. They only make up about 0.1 percent of all Blacks but they are richer than all the other Blacks combined.

On traditional cuisine…

Most Blacks eat lots of *mielie pap* (maize meal) because that's all they can afford. Unfortunately the jobless, poor and starving have to eat mielie pap every single day, often without anything like a lamb roast or a steamed lobster to spice it up a bit. On the odd occasion, if they've been able to scratch some money together, they can afford to buy some pig hooves or "walkie talkies" (chicken feet and beaks) to add some flavour and variety to their pap, but I don't think those are quite as flavoursome as a lamb roast.

Aside from the jobless, poor and starving, all other Blacks eat chicken. Blacks love chicken more than any other food. Besides everywhere, the favourite place for Blacks to eat chicken is on a bus. If you've ever travelled by bus in South Africa – which I'd advise you never to do – you'll know that every two hours the bus stops at a petrol station with a fast-food outlet. All the Blacks pile off the bus at these stops and restock their chicken reserves. Once everyone is back on the bus, you can look behind you and see rows of Blacks eating chicken legs and thighs and wings with their hands and smacking their lips regularly. The chicken is best if fried in oil so that it leaves an oily residue on the hands. The grease isn't wiped off with a serviette, but instead it is rubbed into the hands and that's why Blacks never have to buy expensive hand moisturiser. After they're done eating the chicken they toss the bones out the window for a lucky stray dog.

Even BEE magnates' favourite food is chicken. Take a BEE magnate to a 5-star cordon bleu restaurant that serves fillet mignon, crayfish, beluga caviar and abalone and he'll most likely order the quarter chicken and chips. I must be fair, though, and note that some BEE magnates have realised that when dining in a fine establishment with rich Whites and Indians it is frowned upon if they order the rotisserie chicken every time, so sometimes they'll settle for steak. But believe me, they want the chicken. If you ever get in your car and follow a BEE magnate home I guarantee you he'll stop at KFC or Chicken Licken, after which you'll see bones being flung from the window of his speeding BMW.

Other than chicken and mielie pap, Blacks eat foods that other people don't eat – things like sour milk and mouldy bread. Whites have noticed Blacks doing this and out of their natural kindness have come to give all their sour milk and mouldy bread to the Blacks. It's very thoughtful. Other things that Blacks consider to be delicacies are cow's stomach and sheep's head. Since 1994 more Blacks have been attending *braais* (barbeques) hosted by Whites, especially in the cities where racial integration has progressed quite nicely. Even though these Blacks are, for the most part, Black Diamonds, they still enjoy the occasional sheep's head. On more than one occasion I've seen a Black take a sheep's head from a bloody plastic bag and slap it on the griddle at a White's braai. This horrifies Whites because for many Whites it has become fashionable to only eat meat that has been be-headed, de-boned and de-skinned and made to look as little like an animal as possible. So to see an entire sheep's head on a Black's plate while they eat their free-range boneless skinless chicken breasts is, for Whites, most disturbing.

Foods Blacks Eat

On sociability…

On the whole, Blacks are courteous and respectful people. It's amazing how a Black man will bow and allow another man to pass in front of him. Very seldom will you hear a Black shouting in a blind rage, and for the most part they speak nicely to all people. In the Black culture it is a sign of respect to greet someone and ask him how he's doing even if you haven't the foggiest idea who he is. If you look closely, when Blacks walk in the street they will greet every person they pass – similar to the way ants touch feelers when passing each other. Blacks are so courteous and respectful, in fact, that it drives Whites crazy.

Herewith a common telephonic exchange (Black calls White and White answers):

Black says: "Hello, how are you?" (Being respectful and polite.)

White thinks: 'What the hell? Tell me who you are and what you want before you ask me how I am!' (Whites hate it when people act like their friends before they've officially been accepted as such.)

But, instead, White says (brusquely): "Fine, can I help you?"

Black says: "I'm also fine." (Even though White didn't ask.) "You are speaking to Sipho Ndlovu."

White thinks: 'I don't care how you are or what your name is, just tell me what the hell you want.'

But, instead, White says (more brusquely): "Can I help you?"

Black says: "Can I speak to Sophie please?" (Sophie is Sipho's wife.)

White thinks: 'Well why on earth didn't you just say so in the first place?'

But, instead, White says: "Hold on, I'll go call her."

Most Blacks are best friends with each other, even though they've never met. And they would be best friends with Whites if Whites weren't so scared of Blacks. Often a Black will be walking in the road and he'll suddenly find himself walking alongside another Black. They'll start talking about all sorts of things, like the weather and their children and the weekend's soccer scores. They'll eventually say goodbye and never see each other again, but they'll always be friends. Sometimes a Black man will even hold hands with another Black man while they're talking, and apparently this is not a sign of being gay.

Blacks also love to shout across any expanse of space to greet their friends who, as we've established, are all other Blacks. They can be in the street, in a busy grocery store or even at a restaurant and they'll roar greetings across the room to all the other Blacks. You can be sitting at your table and the next thing you'll hear this person shout at the top of his voice, "Hello! How are you?" To which the Black on the opposite side of the restaurant will reply, "Hello, fine. How are you?" Quite likely this will be in some tribal language like Venda or Zulu or French. And they'll proceed to talk about everything that has happened in their lives in the last two years, in their loudest voices, with you sandwiched in between them. Whites think this is very rude.

On job satisfaction...

Blacks are actually a lot of fun and, boy, do they love to socialise. If you drive through any nice suburb in the afternoon you'll see little groups of maids in their blue and pink maids' outfits, sitting on the grass. They sit for hours, until the sun sets, chatting and laughing and eating chicken and rubbing chicken oil into their hands.

Because they love to socialise so much, Blacks often congregate in groups at work and this drives their employers crazy. It often results in them not doing their jobs properly or efficiently. For example, if you go to the airport you're bound to see immigration officials or security personnel standing in little pockets, just chatting and laughing and having a roaring old time, while an Asian man sails through the checkpoint with 84 pairs of fake Levi's jeans in his suitcase.

Usually when the Blacks are standing in these pockets there is a lone ranger who is still working, which is another interesting thing about Blacks – they love to watch others work. Next time you walk past a construction site, have a peek and you'll generally see about twelve Blacks standing in a group chatting and watching while one guy digs a trench.

When the White foreman spots this scene he typically has a minor heart attack and storms out of his prefabricated office with his hard hat sliding off his head, swearing and shouting at the Blacks to do some bloody work. In obedience, the Blacks in the group will gather their pickaxes and help the lone ranger to dig the trench but the White boss will carry on standing there and give them a spitting lecture. The lecture usually takes the form of a succession of rhetorical questions like, "What the hell, do you think I'm running a charity here? How many times do I have to tell you to get back to work? Don't you take any bloody pride in your work? When you stand around and do nothing you're stealing from the company, you know? Is that what you want? Huh? Is it? Do you want to be called a thief?"

After the lecture, the boss must make a decision depending on the Blacks' reactions. If the Blacks appear to have learnt their lesson and are digging the trench with passion, he'll walk back to his prefabricated house, satisfied that he's motivated them to work. However, if the Blacks are not showing enough remorse and are purposefully digging slowly (working slowly is a tool commonly used by Blacks to drive their bosses crazy and it's officially called a "go-slow") then the boss has to up the stakes. He'll say something like, "I don't know why I don't fire the lot of you. How stupid and lazy are you? Get out of there and let me show you how to dig a bloody trench."

The boss will then push all thirteen Blacks (including the lone ranger) out of the trench and tell them to watch how it's done. He'll grab a pickaxe and start vigorously hacking at the earth, digging and digging until his face is red and he's sweating like a pig. Once he climbs out of the trench he's so tired he can't speak and he goes back to his prefabricated office, whether the Blacks start digging passionately or not.

Whether they're working, socialising in a group, or being shouted at by the boss, Blacks are almost always smiling. Blacks love to smile and laugh and it is quite a wonderful thing. Upon returning to South Africa after a long absence the smiles on the faces of the Blacks are so refreshing and infectious that you can't help but feel happy yourself. This is especially apparent when you've just returned from a place like London, where everyone has such a glum look on their face you'd think their whole family was just taken hostage by FARC guerrillas in Columbia.

All that smiling means their teeth are often exposed, and I always used to wonder how Blacks got such brilliant, white teeth, especially because they love sugar so much. If you drive through a sugar cane region you'll see fields of Blacks gnawing at stalks of sugar cane, yet when they smile and wave as you drive past, their teeth are as white as snow. Also, my friend has this maid and she has the teeth of a beauty queen even though she takes her coffee with fifteen teaspoons of sugar. (They actually almost fired her because they noticed the sugar was being rapidly depleted and they thought she was stealing it. Have you ever?) I honestly don't know how they do it.

But now that I think about it, maybe their teeth look so white because they contrast with their brown skin. I reckon if you put those teeth on a White they wouldn't look as great, which makes me think maybe that's why the British seem to have such horrendous teeth – when your skin is as white as that guy in that movie *Powder*, it's pretty hard to get your teeth to appear white. That said, a pasty complexion can explain away the gross colour, but it doesn't explain why their teeth are all shooting off in different directions. I mean, I've seen some British people whose teeth actually grow *behind* one another – their mouths look like a great white shark's. I once saw this guy whose bottom incisors were all lined up behind one another and he had these canines that stuck out under his top lip even with his mouth shut. And I'm not joking here, his one top incisor was almost double the size of the other – I've never seen such a revolting mouth in all my life. Seriously, I actually had to look away when he talked to me. Anyway, I'm getting sidetracked here but the point is, for whatever reason, Blacks generally have good-looking teeth and I know this because they smile a lot.

On technology…

Because a lot of Blacks grew up in poverty, many of them haven't been exposed to much technology. But they're learning fast. They can use computers and other gadgets as well as anyone else, but there is still one thing they struggle with: dialling the correct number on a cellphone. Blacks are always dialling the wrong number. It's become so bad that many people don't answer their phones when they see a number they don't recognise. Instead they let it go to voice mail because, if they were to answer, the first thing they would hear is "Hello, how are you?"

On accents…

Blacks don't speak English at home but on the whole they've grasped the English language pretty well. Most Blacks speak English with a Black accent, which is difficult to explain in a book but if you hear a Black speak English you'll know what a Black accent sounds like. They say things like "vowlence" when they mean violence, and "wek" when they mean work.

Furthermore, Blacks haven't quite grasped the terms "in two weeks' time" or "two years ago". Instead of saying "in two weeks' time" Blacks will say "next of next week", or if they want to tell you that something happened three years ago they will say it happened "last of last of last year". It's a peculiar way of talking but once you understand what they're saying it's pretty easy to work out.

On sport...

Blacks mostly love one sport: soccer. Black children in townships and homelands are always playing soccer, but never with a proper ball. They're always playing with an old tennis ball or a punctured volleyball or a rolled-up pair of trousers. If I were them and I loved soccer so much I would get a decent ball, for goodness sake.

Occasionally you will get a Black who ventures so far as to play golf or tennis, but this is very risky for a Black. Other Blacks don't like it when Blacks play these sports because they feel they're trying to be White, and the tennis-playing Black will be taunted with comments about forgetting his roots. Blacks who play golf or tennis are called Coconuts because they are black on the outside and white on the inside.

Coconuts can also be Blacks who speak English without a Black accent. Aspiring Coconuts know that if they hang around Blacks their entire lives they're never going to lose their Black accent. So to get a White accent a Black will usually attend a posh private school where there are lots of Whites. Whites are very impressed with Blacks who speak English without a Black accent. They say things like, "My my, that Black Boy speaks so well. He sounds just like us." On the whole, it's not a good thing to be a Coconut because Blacks are sceptical of the loyalty of Coconuts; and Whites like Coconuts simply because they are the token Blacks that help them appear racially accepting. Whites love to appear racially accepting.

On stress and time management...

Blacks have no stress. Whites stress about everything – careers, money, getting hurt, dying, dirty feet on the carpet, you name it. Blacks are relaxed from the moment they're born until the day they die. If Blacks get tired or a little stressed for some reason, they just go sleep in the shade of a tree, using a rolled-up jacket as a pillow. They'll sleep soundly, even if there is a shoot-out taking place across the street between the police and cash-in-transit robbers. When the Black is sufficiently rested he'll go back to whatever he was doing. When maids or gardeners do this it infuriates their bosses because they get paid a whole R12 for the hour they were sleeping and by sleeping on the job the Blacks are stealing from them.

Blacks only wear watches because they look flashy – many Blacks don't even realise when their watch batteries go flat because they never look at their watches. They don't look at their watches because the time Blacks follow is called Africa Time and Africa Time cannot be kept on a watch. Africa Time is actually not even kept because it never runs out. With Africa Time there is always time. Whites think that time runs out, which is why they're always in such a rush. But according to Africa Time, if there's no time today then there will be time tomorrow and the next day and the next day. This is why Blacks never rush anything.

Stressed Black

(Doesn't Exist)

On the beach...

Blacks love the beach. They roll around on the sand, getting it all in their underclothes, and they run around and play soccer and dance and sing and splash in the waves. When you see how much Blacks love the beach you wonder why they only go once a year – on New Year's Day. No-one fully understands it, but on New Year's Day Blacks swarm to the beach like lemmings controlled by an inexplicable urge to get to the ocean. They descend on the beaches in hundreds and thousands all over the country in minibus taxis and buses and old Toyota Cressidas. Whites are well aware of this and that's why you'll never see a White on the beach on New Year's Day. (If you think you saw a White on the beach on New Year's Day it was actually an Albino, which is a Black who has white skin. This confuses some people but Albinos are also Blacks even though they have white skin because they speak English with a Black accent and have above-average-sized lips and curly hair.)

There are two small problems with Blacks going to the beach. Firstly, they can't swim. And secondly, no beach in the world is big enough to accommodate two hundred thousand people. So what happens is the swarms of lemming-like Blacks arrive at the beach and take off their clothes and run into the ocean in their holey underwear. When they're in the ocean the swarms behind them push them further and further until it's too deep to stand and then they have to be rescued by the lifeguards.

On getting on with animals...

Blacks don't get on at all well with animals. For one, dogs hate them, especially if the dog belongs to a White. A White can walk past someone's house and their dog will run to the gate with a tennis ball in its mouth, begging to be played with. It will allow the White to stroke it and pat its head and jiggle the flap of skin under its chin. But don't even think of trying that if you're a Black. A Black can be walking along and a hundred metres before he gets to the house, the dog will start snarling and growling at the fence. The Black can walk past the house on the opposite side of the road but the dog will bark and growl and snarl and try to jam its head through a hole in the fence to attack the Black. If the owners are home they'll come out and see the Black walking past and watch him until he's out of sight, thinking their dog was barking because the Black was trying to break in. The White will then reinforce this behaviour by patting the dog's head and saying, "There's a good dog, you're a good watchdog." And all the Black was doing was walking to the shop. It's very unfair really. Sometimes dogs can be such racists.

The other animal that Blacks don't get along with is lions in the Kruger National Park, but I don't think the lions are racists like the dogs. The lions just eat the Blacks because they're walking from Mozambique to South Africa and when a lion spots an easy kill, it'll take it. We can't yet prove if the lions are racists because there are no Whites walking through the Kruger Park.

But the animal Blacks hate most is a snake because they believe snakes are evil. You just have to say the word *nyoka* (which means snake in tribal language), and any Blacks in your immediate vicinity will break into a sweat and say *How how how!* (which means I am very scared right now). There has never been a Black snake handler and there never will be. Ever. A guy I knew once had a rubber snake and he put it half under the couch with its head protruding and yanked it out with some fishing line when his maid walked past. She screamed her head off and jumped so high she almost hit the ceiling and then she didn't come back to work for a week, which was a catastrophe because the house got into such a mess. This is a true story.

On communism...
Blacks are the most generous and sharing people I know and we can learn a lot from them. The reason we don't learn from

them is because we learned from the Russians that sharing is another name for communism, and communism makes people depressed and causes you to get to the moon in second place.

I think Blacks' sharing attitude comes from the traditional tribal structure where there is one chief and all the land belongs to the collective people, and everyone lives together and shares what they have. If there is food, everyone eats and if there is no food, no-one eats. Examples of this are everywhere. You will seldom see a car with one Black in it because they always give lifts to each other (except for BEE magnates and politicians – they never give lifts to anyone). Many maids and gardeners support an entire family on the money they make and sometimes they also have to look after their extended families, yet they bear it with a smile.

This sense of community runs very deep with Blacks. My friend's maid told me that if your neighbour has two chickens and you have none then one of those chickens is yours. You don't even have to ask if you can have it – it's yours to take. That's because everything is for all to share and it is the main reason why most of Africa doesn't have property rights; the land belongs to all the people collectively. Whites have a different philosophy – they prefer to have their own things. This poses a problem for the Blacks because some of them get shocked by electric fences when climbing over the White's walls to retrieve their share of the chickens.

Another thing Blacks love to share is personal space. A Black will join a queue at the ATM, jamming his chest into the spine of the person in front of him. He'll stand so close you can hear his uvula vibrating in the back of his throat as he breathes. Even if it's a sweltering day, when some space would help keep you cool, the Black will push his torso against your back and think nothing of it. This irritates Whites because all Whites have a two-metre space bubble around them that is their private property and if anyone enters that bubble they're trespassing and they need to back away.

Blacks Trespassing on Whites' Personal Space

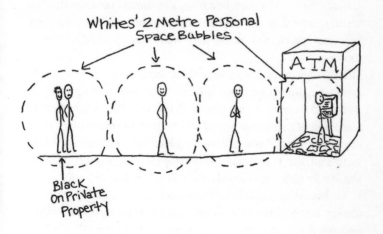

Whites' 2 Metre Personal Space Bubbles

ATM

Black on Private Property

On the men...

Black men are actually adults and not boys. It's necessary to state this fact because some Whites call Blacks "boy". I'm not really sure why but it's not uncommon to hear a 16-year-old White kid call a 63-year-old Black man "boy", even though the Black man is 47 years older than him and has five children and eleven grandchildren.

Having clarified that, did you know that Black men spend more money on shoes every month than any other demographic, including White and Black women? This is because Black men are very image conscious. The most important things to a Black man are his two sets of wheels – one set being his car and the other being his shoes. If you go to a fancy bar the Black men are always wearing the nicest shoes.

In general, Black men dress very well. They love expensive

brand-name clothes. If you go to the townships you'll see men walking along the side of the road dressed in suits and shiny black shoes. And even the maids dress well when they go out. Usually they're just seen in a maid's uniform but when they go to the shops they put on their best clothes and they do their hair and rub chicken fat on their hands and get really snazzy-looking.

All Black guys would give their left foot to have a White girlfriend. But despite being so well dressed, getting a White girlfriend is very tough for a Black man in South Africa. Unfortunately, the majority of White girls don't find Black men attractive. On the odd occasion a Black man will land a White girlfriend, but that usually only happens to Coconuts because the White girls who would date a Black guy would only do so if he doesn't speak with a Black accent. Also, he has to have money because White girls don't want to go to the township and eat mielie pap in a shack when visiting the Black man's parents.

The other option Black men have if they want to land a White chick is to go to Germany. German women go berserk for Black men because they are known for having big feet and German women love men with big feet. But sadly for them, most Blacks don't take their holidays in continental Europe so they never get to exercise their advantage in a place like Germany.

Most Black men are very lean and strong and fit, especially the ones that dig trenches and work in gardens. Some people look at them and are jealous of their great bodies. But when they realise a diet of mielie pap and an exercise regime consisting of digging in the hot sun all day is what's needed to look like that, they say they can keep it. The Black Diamonds are pretty varied in shape and the politicians and BEE magnates are all fat because they laze around in offices all day and eat KFC after dinners with Whites and Indians.

On the women…

Some Black women, like those from Kenya and Tanzania, have slim and athletic-looking bodies like Indians or Whites. But South African Black chicks sure don't have those kinds of bodies. They have big bums and big boobs and big thighs, and they have concave calves. This is just the way Black men like them. I asked my Black friend once if he liked that chick over there from Tanzania and he said no, she needed to get a bigger bum. Just as well Black men like their women big and curvy, because if not, Black women would be up the creek without a paddle.

You'd think that Black women would wear clothes that would soften the lines of their bodies, but they don't. They wear the tightest-fitting clothes they can find. Take jeans, for example. It must take some Black women a full hour to get into their jeans, and when they're on, the jeans hug every curve and bulge like a sackful of oranges. When one of these chicks walks past you in her tight-fitting clothes and high heels, you can't help but stare. It's like a car accident – you feel you shouldn't look but you can't stop yourself. And then when you think she couldn't fit anything else into those pants, you spot a cellphone stuffed in the back pocket.

Black women don't have long straight hair like White or Indian women, so they need to use hair products to straighten their hair. Lots and lots of hair products. Black chicks spend millions of rands on these products every year and it's quite clear that the major ingredient in these products is oil. Actually, I don't think there's anything *but* oil and possibly a little cheap perfume in those products – you may as well buy a pint of Castrol GTX motor oil and rub that on your head. These products give Black chicks' hair an oily sheen that makes me think of an otter's coat. Black men love this look.

The Wonders of Hair Products

MOTOR OIL + CHEAP PERFUME = HAIR PRODUCT

BEFORE PRODUCT

AFTER PRODUCT

Black women cannot drive. You should avoid being in the vicinity of a Black chick in her car at all times. If you're driving on the highway and you come up behind a Black chick in a car you should back off immediately and take the nearest exit to avert the danger. Black women are easy to spot in cars by the following:

> There is a pair of DD boobs on the dashboard.

> The car is going 45km/h in the fast lane of the highway.

> Smoke is coming out from under the bonnet because she's still in first gear.

> Every bumper has a dent.

> She's typing an SMS on her cellphone while sipping some water while applying lip gloss while talking to her friend.

One thing Black women can do like nobody else is dance. And boy do they love it – especially when they're in a group of four or more. If a song comes on the radio the Black women will all go "Woo woo woo!" and get up and start dancing and singing along to the tune and clapping their hands and laughing uncontrollably. And they really can dance – those big hips and bums move as if they have a mind of their own. Even the lemon-faced looks from disapproving Whites won't deter them.

If Blacks are dancing and singing in this fashion and a White drives past, the White will usually look and sneer, thinking the Blacks are rioting. Whites don't like it when Blacks riot. In their defence, Whites can be forgiven for thinking the Blacks are rioting when they see some Black women dancing and singing on the side of the road. Why, you ask? Because, oddly enough, when Blacks get angry they dance. And sing. It's the most bizarre thing ever. If a whole factory of Blacks lose their jobs or don't get decent wage increases, they don't shout and curse and plot to murder the boss. Instead, they go out into the street and they dance like crazy for days on end. They also sing at the tops of their voices and for the entire time they have huge smiles on their faces. They must be the happiest disgruntled people in the world. This practice is also known as *toyi-toying*. So Whites are usually not sure if the Blacks are just enjoying a song on the radio or if they're rioting.

Black guys love nothing more than to come across a group of Black women who are dancing, and when given half a chance they quickly join them. Once the Black guys join the circle though, the nature of the dancing changes. Where previously it was a hip-shaking, arms-waving, finger-clicking, laughter-filled dance, it now becomes an act called "grinding". The Black men will just stand with their pelvises pushed forward while the women reverse their bums up against their pelvises. The man will put his hands on the woman's hips and she'll bend forward and rest her hands on her knees for support. The look on her face will change from glee to seduction. Then she will shake and move her bum up and down and side to side, and that's grinding. Blacks love to grind but if you're not a Black you may think it's dodgy.

Needless to say, with their big bums and grinding capabilities, Black chicks are in high demand with Black guys. So much so that when they decide to marry them, the men will actually buy the bride from the bride's father. Please note: this is not considered human trafficking, it is just an ancient tradition called *lobola*. Traditionally the father asks for a certain number of cattle to be paid in exchange for the bride. It doesn't make much sense to me to exchange a bunch of cows for one cow, but hey, if they want to do it, it doesn't make any difference to my life.

Chapter 2:
WHITES
(White English-speaking people)

On making the rules…

Whites love rules and laws – but only if they get to make them. Whites want to make the rules for one reason: they hate other people telling them what to do. That's why they hate car guards so much – because they're always telling you what to do. The moment you drive into a parking lot the car guards all start flailing their arms, telling you to stop and wait and go and slow down and park over here and listen to me whistle and give me two rand my boss – it drives Whites crazy.

Because they so badly want to make the rules, many Whites spend their lives trying to become the boss of a corporate company or the owner of their own business so *they* can tell others what to do. Said another way, if you get to make the rules you don't have to follow them. One of the best examples of the rules Whites like to make is "The customer is always right". This rule is such torture for employees because, more often than not, the customer is not actually right. But because the rule says so, the customer *is* right and that makes the lowly employee, who is usually Black or Coloured, wrong by default.

As soon as they become the boss, Whites immediately get started on their favourite task: making up rules for their employees. Once they've compiled their list of rules, they'll turn it into a "Policies and Procedures Document". This document is the boss's rule book and it teaches the employees to act more like robot zombies and less like humans. White bosses prefer robot zombies to humans because robot zombies make fewer mistakes and mistakes cost money. Also, humans have other opinions and other opinions are always wrong.

At work the Policies and Procedures Document is the law and everybody must abide by it. For example, if an employee falls off the roof of his house while trying to retrieve a little girl's stranded cat and breaks both legs, his jaw and his nose, and cracks three vertebrae in his lower back, the policy will determine how he is treated by his employer. From his hospital bed the employee will phone his White boss and say, "Boss, I broke both my legs, my jaw and my nose, and I have three cracked vertebrae in my lower back. Please may I have three weeks to recover in hospital?"

Emotionless, the boss will reply, "Well, I'll have to check our policy on that." And he'll check the policy (even though he doesn't really have to) and it will say employees only get one week of sick leave and thereafter they must take unpaid leave. The boss will then call the employee back and say, "Sorry, I checked the policy and you can only have one week off."

And the employee says, "But I'm practically dying here, man! Don't you have an ounce of sympathy?"

"Sorry, that's what the policy says," the boss replies.

"But who makes the policy?"

"I do."

"Well, then why can't you change it? I fell off a roof. I'm completely immobile here!"

"I can't change it because it's the same for everyone. It would be unfair to change it for one person."

"Well it might be fair in that everyone gets the same, but if it's a kick in the face with an ice skate – which is what this is – then that's not exactly a good thing, is it?"

"Sorry there's nothing I can do."

"Yes there is! You can change the policy. You're the boss!"

"Well, actually I can't change the policy because the policy says you need to follow the correct channels if you want to change the policy. So if you have a complaint you need to speak to someone in HR."

"Okay, well then transfer me to HR."

The boss transfers him to Human Resources and, after listening to the complaint, the consultant says (in a nutshell), "Thank you for your call. We can escalate this complaint but it'll take three months to resolve so there's probably no point anyway."

By now transcendentally frustrated, the employee tries one last time to appeal to someone's humanity: "But can't you help me somehow?"

And the consultant says, "Sorry, there's nothing on helping in the policy."

"Argh!" the employee exclaims, slamming down the phone. If he'd ever had any dealings with the Policies and Procedures Document in the past, he'd have known not to waste his time in the first place and just accepted being poor and physically incapacitated for the foreseeable future.

It's important to note that the White boss does, at times, relax the rules. Most White bosses have done this by introducing something called "Casual Friday". Casual Friday is a day (almost always a Friday) when robot zombies are exempted from the dress-code rule, which requires them to dress respectably at work. Casual Friday is a great idea which gives the employees the chance to wear their favourite casual clothes to the office. Afrikaners slip on their two-tone shirts and rugby jerseys, Indian women get to drape saris over themselves, Black chicks wear their figure-hugging jeans and Black guys get to show off their favourite wheels. Also, Casual Friday allows the White boss to create the impression that he cares as much about the happiness of his employees as he does about making money and making rules.

Some White bosses will dress down like everyone else on Casual Friday, but mostly they don't because they still want to distinguish themselves from the robot zombies as the lawmakers. So they usually just wear the same smart clothes, but without a tie. Sadly, some companies have stopped Casual Fridays because employees seem to think that when they're exempt from wearing work clothes they're also exempt from working. When the White boss notices that the employees are doing no work on Fridays he'll send an email to the whole company, cancelling Casual Friday. He'll scold them for abusing their privileges – because wearing casual clothes to work is such a privilege – and berate them for "taking a whole arm when he gave them a finger". The cancellation of Casual Friday is devastating for robot zombies… just devastating.

On how to be the boss…

According to Whites, to become the boss a person requires only one thing: ambition. For Whites, ambition is the single most honourable attribute in a human being. That's why if you want to pay a White the worst insult ever, just ask him in a patronising, rhetorical tone, "Have you no ambition?"

But be careful. Asking a White this will make him spitting mad because people who have no ambition end up working as car guards or driving tow-trucks. From a young age Whites are taught to be ambitious, to figure out what they want out of life and to go for it. At school, little children of six and seven are asked what they want to be one day. Children who answer "a lawyer", "an accountant", "a doctor", "an engineer" or "a billionaire badass property tycoon" are commended. Their teachers applaud their good choices and they tell them they'll go far in life with such ambition. However, children who give answers like "a surfer", "a glass blower", "a director of skateboarding videos" or "I don't know" are ridiculed and asked the question, "Child, have you no ambition?"

Because they value ambition so highly, Whites consider men like Donald Trump and Bill Gates among the world's greatest people. Or, even better, Richard Branson. Almost all Whites aspire to be Richard Branson because not only did he build a billion-dollar empire, but he also knows how to fly a hot-air balloon. And even though most Whites admire philanthropists like Gandhi and Mother Teresa, they don't really want to be like them because Gandhi and Mother Teresa didn't have enough ambition to build an empire from their philanthropic pursuits. They didn't even have a big fancy house with an SUV and a station wagon parked in the drive and a nice garden with a swimming pool and an electric fence and two Labradors and some children running around.

From early on, White parents will monitor the development of their child's ambition. If, by the age of four, the parents notice that their little Branson-in-the-making is not displaying the required hunger for success, they'll sign him up for a bunch of extracurricular activities, hoping to kick-start a passion for *something*. Unfortunately, this constant pressure has the exact opposite effect: the child loses all ambition as he sees clearly what ambition did to his parents. Pretty soon his only passion in life is to play video games and even then he isn't really too bothered if he wins or loses.

Thankfully, after years of trying to ignite some passion in their kids, most parents submit to the fact that their child is simply not ambitious enough to ever fly hot-air balloons while the billions roll in. This is the precise moment at which they decide to enrol the child at a private school. Private schools serve the interests of two types of children:

1. Ambitious children who want to be challenged to become the best at the elected object of their ambition.

2.   Children with no ambition who have been sent to a private school to build camaraderie.

Through a fair amount of fake smiling, back slapping*, being agreeable in every conceivable way and calling each other bugger, my boy, old boy and boychie, camaraderie is built between boys at private schools. This camaraderie ensures that one day the ambitionless ones will get jobs with the ambitious ones just because they went to the same school.

*A note on back slapping: It is important to realise that back slapping as a tool for building camaraderie is much different to the kind of back slapping used to dislodge a chicken bone from someone's throat. Camaraderie-building back slapping is more like a congratulatory pat, administered to the upper back or shoulders, with an open hand and a fake smile on the face – it helps to imagine you are congratulating the White on being such a fantastic human being because that's exactly what you're doing. This is in stark contrast to the choking-relief back slapping used to dislodge chicken bones, which is more of a hammer punch, repeatedly and vigorously administered with a clenched fist directly between the shoulder blades.

On not quite cutting it...

Sadly for them, a lot of Whites have given up on ever being the boss of somebody else. They've accepted that there are too many dogs fighting over the same bone, so they rather settle into being robot zombies themselves. But fear not! For their ambition is not lost – it's now simply redirected towards other pursuits. These other pursuits include:

> Scuba diving

> Playing golf

> Attending cooking classes

> Taking up fly-fishing

> Taking regular camping and hiking trips

> Travelling to exotic countries like India and Cambodia

> Learning to play a musical instrument

> Learning a new language

> Learning about coffee and wine

> Thinking about writing a book – usually their memoir, about everything they've learnt in life

But the favourite alternative pursuits of Whites-who'll-never-be-the-boss are endurance sports such as running, cycling and canoeing. Each weekend South Africa's roads and rivers are full of ambitious Whites trying to be the best cyclists, runners and canoeists they can be. The Whites become totally obsessed with their endurance sports. Besides practising every day and competing in races on the weekends, their obsession will manifest itself in the following ways:

1. The Whites will subscribe to running, cycling and/or kayaking magazines where they'll read about successful athletes and wish they could be them.

2. The Whites will surf the internet for hours on end in search of shiny new lightweight wickable breathable highly flammable performance-enhancing sports gear.

3. The Whites will buy ludicrously expensive nutritional

supplements and energy gels at pharmacies, health shops and supermarkets.

4.   The Whites will talk about their endurance sport with other White work colleagues, often deliberating over what the foulest tasting energy gel is, for example, and on Casual Friday they'll wear T-shirts acquired at their favourite endurance event.

5.   The Whites will religiously watch major international endurance events on TV, including the Tour de France, the Boston Marathon and the World Canoeing Championships. Secretly they will all dream of some day travelling to one of these events as a spectator or, if they are really ambitious, as a competitor.

The reason Whites like these pursuits so much is that they get to pit themselves against other Whites and gauge their self-worth by comparing speed and times. And because Whites have so much pent-up ambition they take it all very seriously. Really, a Saturday morning ride with a bunch of Whites can be even more cut-throat than a territorial battle between two elephant bulls. And the races are even worse – skirmishes often break out on the road even though the two guys who're fighting are only competing for 4,341st position. Because it takes too much effort to punch or kick someone while you're trying to keep your bicycle upright, the skirmishes are usually just verbal, but that doesn't make them any less vicious. Some of the things Whites say to each other on their bicycles will leave you wondering if there's any love left in the world.

Whites' favourite endurance races in South Africa are:

> Cycling – The Cape Argus, The 94.7 Cycle Challenge, The Cape Epic

> Running – The Comrades Marathon, The Two Oceans Marathon

> Canoeing – The Dusi Canoe Marathon, The Berg Canoe Marathon

Some particularly serious Whites will actually rearrange their whole lives to coincide with their training regime and participation in these races. The shocking thing though is that despite having the same bike as Lance Armstrong, a Polar Heart Rate Monitor and all the other high-performance gadgets money can buy, and being as competitive as it's humanly possible to be, it's not uncommon to see a 50-year-old Black man wearing a three-piece suit and leather shoes cycle past the Whites on the way to his buddy's house on his antique fixed-gear bicycle. And the best part for the Black is that he didn't have to pay a R350 entry fee to cycle the exact same route as the Whites.

One of the main benefits of redirecting one's ambition to an endurance sport like cycling is that at dinner parties, when they're asked how work is going, the Whites don't have to reply with a truthful statement like, "Oh it's awful! But only because I'm somebody who sold his soul to the corporate machine just to pay the bills and I have no opportunity to become the boss, so I've lost all ambition for my job." Despite its honesty, a statement like this will be frowned upon by the other Whites and may lead to the White in question being ostracised and not invited to future dinner parties. But if the White has taken up an alternative pursuit he gets to answer with something like, "How's work? Oh it's pretty relaxed actually. I recently made a lifestyle choice. I decided to become someone who works to live, not someone who lives to work. That's how they do it in Australia. So I just do my time at work and I've now dedicated myself to cycling. So far I've completed three races and in each one I've increased my average speed by one kilometre per hour while keeping my heart rate at an average of 155 beats per minute. I recently switched energy gels which seems to be making a considerable difference to my peak performance and allows me to boost my VO2 max levels to unprecedented heights. It's all about working out what works for *you*. I'm doing my first Argus this weekend and I'm really amped to break three hours. So I'm training super hard for that right now." Being able to provide an answer such as this allows the White to feel terrific about himself while simultaneously maintaining his dignity in the presence of other Whites.

Non-Whites listening to a White go on about his exercise regime are likely to detect an element of smugness in the White's demeanour. Most other Whites don't see it this way, though, and will encourage the exercising White to feel really, really good about himself.

On unknown lawmakers…

Even though they don't really have a clue who he was or what he looked like, Whites are particularly fond of quoting a British master lawmaker named Murphy. Murphy said many things, like "Anything that can possibly go wrong, will go wrong" and "No good deed goes unpunished", and all the things he said are collectively known as Murphy's Law. For example, if you drop your piece of buttered bread on the floor a White will usually nod knowingly and say, "Yep, that's Murphy's Law. Whenever you drop a piece of bread on the floor it lands on the buttered side." Murphy's Law neither helps you to prevent your bread from falling on the buttered side, nor does it help you to pick it up, but Whites love to tell you what he said anyway.

Hundreds of years ago Murphy also said, "Whoever has the gold, makes the rules." The British people took this particular law to heart and they sailed the world in search of gold, accumulating as much as they could, so that they could make many more rules. And that's why they came to South Africa in the late 1800s – to get gold and make rules.

On being excellent miners…

The interesting thing is that gold isn't good enough any more. These days they want platinum (I'm referring to White women here). Gold isn't good enough any more because White women discovered that platinum costs more than gold and they say they don't want jewellery that's cheap. (Trying to explain to them that gold is, in fact, not cheap is pointless.)

Because White women have always loved gold so much some of them have been branded Gold Diggers. Gold Digger is a term that describes a woman who only goes for men with money so she can get nice things from them, like leather boots and fake boobs. The term confused me before I knew what it meant, because I've seen hundreds of photos taken inside mine shafts and I've never seen a White woman laying dynamite or taking a jackhammer to a rock face.

Now that they prefer platinum, I think White women should rather be called Platinum Diggers. Or maybe Diamond Diggers, because even a platinum ring isn't good enough unless it's got a big glittering diamond glued on top of it. White women are obsessed with diamonds. This doesn't make much sense to me because the big shiny diamonds they love so much serve no purpose whatsoever, besides looking pretty and enticing would-be muggers. It would be far wiser to get something useful like an industrial diamond, because at least you can *do* something with an industrial diamond, like cut through glass. Even more useful is something like a Leatherman multi-purpose tool. Yes, if I were a White woman I would definitely go for a Leatherman, because you can pretty much do anything with a Leatherman. And when worn on your belt in a black canvas pouch, a Leatherman actually attracts more attention than a little diamond on your finger.

Anyhow, I don't think that craze will ever take off, no matter how much I like the idea, because White women are dead set on the platinum ring with a diamond. My friend tried to get away with buying his fiancée a white-gold engagement ring, which is gold that's been polished to look like platinum, but even that wasn't good enough. He lied to her (in hindsight, a poor decision) and told her it was platinum but she took it to a jeweller to get it verified and the jeweller told her it was white gold. Boy was she angry! When she got back home she pulled the ring off and threw it at him and told him if he wanted to marry her he better cough up. She also said she wasn't going to let him get away with buying her "cheap trash" (even though it was neither cheap nor trash). So he had to go back to the jeweller and get a platinum housing for the diamond and only then was she happy. She is a Gold Digger. Or a Platinum Digger. Whatever, you know what I mean. And now she's asking him for a pair of fake boobs, which don't come cheap either.

By the way, many White women will get their engagement rings verified and appraised at a jeweller, or at the very least they will seriously consider it. That's something to remember if you ever plan on marrying a White woman.

On bending the rules…

In accordance with Murphy's Law, with their platinum rings on their fingers, White women get to make the rules at home. And they can make their husbands' lives a living hell if they want to, so White men must tread very lightly. Needless to say, they are terrified of their wives. Really, they are.

I know this one guy who swears like a trooper when he's with his buddies but as soon as his wife is around he talks like an angel. Seriously, when she's next to him he doesn't say anything unless it's encouraging, uplifting, kind, loving or happy. She's even got him to talk with her in baby talk. I mean have you ever, in your life, heard two adults talking to one another like babies? It's disgusting. One time us guys were all watching rugby at his house and swearing and shouting at the TV when his wife walks into the room and the next thing he's talking to her like she's six months old, calling her buggerlugs and boogiebear and saying peek-a-boo I see you and other such demeaning things. And then she starts talking to him in a squeaky voice like he's *also* six months old, asking him if he wants some nana or a bottie or a blankie and tugging at his puffy cheeks. Seriously, it was so appalling I can barely stand to think about it. And then – no jokes – the second she leaves the room he starts spraying insults and swear words again like a Tommy gun, saying things like eff the state of South African rugby and just get me another effing beer, when a second ago it was buggerlugs and boogiebear. Boy that guy is terrified of his wife.

I'm not altogether surprised she got him to speak baby talk with her because White women are notorious for threatening hell on earth to get what they want out of their husbands. Besides baby talk, the things White women want most is for their husbands to *desire* to wash the dishes and to *desire* to snuggle with them on the couch on a Friday night and watch a Hugh Grant romantic comedy. What White women don't realise is that no man on planet Earth *desires* to wash dishes or watch those kinds of movies on a Friday night. But they try to make them desire it anyway, using two methods:

1. Sex rationing

White men, like all men, love to have sex. White women know this so they become more miserly in allocating them sex-time unless the husband shows some desire to wash the dishes or watch Hugh Grant movies. It's a bit like an owner training her dog. She commands the dog to roll over, and if the dog obeys she gives it a biscuit. If it doesn't roll over it doesn't get a biscuit. Many White men still struggle to identify the roll-over-and-get-a-biscuit principle when it arises and this leads to confusion and frustration. Let me explain.

It's Friday night and White husband wants some sex and makes a move on his wife. White wife is unhappy because White husband grumbled when washing the dishes earlier that evening. White wife decides she's going to refuse White husband sex until he learns to wash the dishes with a smile on his face. So White wife tells White husband she has a headache. White husband says he has just the thing for her and runs to get her a headache tablet. White wife refuses to take the headache tablet because she says it won't work. White husband reasons that the other day she had a headache and she took a headache tablet and it made her feel right as rain. White wife says this is a different kind of headache and tablets don't work for these kinds of headaches. White husband says well he didn't know there were different kinds of headaches but he bets if she took the tablet she would feel better. (By this stage White husband is really champing at the bit for some sex.) White wife snaps back at him and says it won't work because she has a fatigue headache from all the housework she's been doing and tablets don't work for fatigue headaches. White husband says but he washed the dishes that evening. White wife says that didn't count because he was grumbling while he did it and until he learns to wash dishes with a smile on his face her headache won't go away. And White husband eventually gets the message. It's a pretty roundabout way of getting the point across but for some reason White wives persist with it.

2. Making more rules

White women use their authority to make thousands of rules for their husbands. Every time the husband fails to read the wife's mind and do what she expects of him, she slaps on another rule. Common examples of rules are:

> No working late

> No drinking after golf

> No food in the bedroom

> No dirty feet on the couch

> No fishing on our beach holiday

> No kissing me until you've shaved

> No watching rugby until the lawn is mowed

> No peeing standing up in the middle of the night. Make sure you sit down so you don't wake me up and you don't widdle on the floor…

After some time White men learn to abide by the rules and they realise that by doing so the wife is happier and she rewards him with more sex rations and occasionally with something called a pink slip. A pink slip is an imaginary authorisation document a wife gives her husband that entitles him to go out with his friends. Even though he can go out with his friends, he must be sure not to return home drunk or smelling like alcohol, otherwise he won't see another pink slip for a long, long time.

Usually when the husband returns home from a pink-slip outing he wants to have some sex, but if she detects even the remotest scent of alcohol or cigarettes he doesn't stand a chance. The only way he'll get sex after a pink-slip outing is if he returns home before his curfew with a bunch of flowers and he smells like popcorn, because he went to watch a movie with his buddies and it was a non-violent thought-provoking movie, preferably starring Hugh Grant.

On thirst…

Going out with their buddies without drinking is just torturous for White guys because they simply can't resist a drink on a night out. White guys can seldom limit themselves to one or two drinks when they're out. Instead they prefer to get piss drunk. Especially in their youth. Besides loving the feeling of being piss drunk, young White guys get piss drunk for two reasons.

Firstly, they do stupid things and this, according to them, is a good thing. The top six stupid things they do when they get piss drunk are:

1. Drive

2. Call an ex-lover at 3am and ask her to come out

3. Go to a strip club

4. Spend R1,000 buying drinks for strangers

5. Eat McDonald's

6. Dive into a bush. (Otherwise known as bush-diving)

The second reason White guys like to get piss drunk is that being able to get really drunk is both a declaration of masculinity and it helps to build camaraderie. For White guys, the more you drink and the drunker you get, the more of a man you are. For example, you'll often hear White guys using war metaphors to describe their friends' drinking antics. They'll say things like "Greg was wasted by 10 o'clock but he soldiered on until 3am", or "Andy is such a warrior – that guy never stops drinking".

Usually the White guys will all gather together on the morning after a night of heavy drinking and laugh in croaky voices as they swap stories about how drunk they got. This kind of behaviour is perplexing to Black and Coloured men because in their cultures getting the drunkest is not always a sign of manhood – it may in fact be a sign of foolishness. This is not to say Blacks and Coloureds don't get drunk. Far from it. But they seldom get drunk and dive into bushes then talk about it the next day like they won the lottery or something.

The pinnacle of any White's drunken story is if he vomited – that really cracks the rest of the Whites up. And even better than simply vomiting is if he vomited on himself or in somebody else's car. The Whites who witnessed the vomiting will candidly relay the story to all who were not present. For example:

"Hey Mike, you know Steve McAlpine? Remember him from varsity? We were out on Friday night and we got so smashed, man, it was freakin' awesome! We jammed until the club closed at like 4am. So anyway, on the way home old McAlpine vomits all over the back seat of Dave Stewart's new Audi. It was the funniest thing ever! Ah man, I wish you could've seen it! Dave got so angry he started swearing at McAlpine, but McAlpine was too wasted to know what was going on. I thought he was gonna kick him out of the car right there on the highway. But instead – get this! – he opens the rear window and makes McAlpine hang his head out the window all the way home. McAlpine looked like a dog with his head out the window and his tongue hanging out. And when we got home there was vomit all over the inside *and* outside of Dave's car. Oh man, Dave was so hacked off he started scrubbing his car seats as soon as we got home and the whole time he's swearing and telling McAlpine he's never riding with him again while McAlpine starts bush diving into Dave's hedge. Eventually we got to bed and woke up the next day at, like, four in the afternoon with the worst hangovers ever. But it was so worth it!"

And Mike will respond with something like, "What? McAlpine did that? For real? No way! Oh man, McAlpine is such a legend. That dude is all class."

Besides using the term piss drunk, Whites will often use substitute words which mean the same thing. It's important to remember these words so you can know what the White is talking about when he tells you his drunken story. For example, instead of saying he got piss drunk a White might say he got wasted, rat-faced, rat-arsed, blazed, broken, slammed, smashed, bent, hammered, tanked, totalled, torn or Cape Malayed.

On romance…

White chicks, like Black chicks, love to dance (although White chicks won't dance in the streets when they're disgruntled). Most Friday nights, groups of White chicks get dressed in skimpy outfits and doll themselves up to look more beautiful than they actually are. Then they go to nightclubs and throw their bags and jackets in a little pile on the floor and huddle in groups around the pile and do their dancing with their backs turned to everyone else. It's somewhat insular if you ask me.

There's just one problem. White chicks can't dance. Black chicks get their bums and hips to move to the music as if they have a mind of their own but White chicks can't manage to do this – they have to think about their dance moves and practise them so their dancing always appears a tad forced. That's why if you see a White dancing next to a Black, the White looks like she has rigor mortis while the Black moves like she's made of grape-flavoured jelly.

Thankfully for the Whites though, not many Blacks go to the same nightclubs as Whites so you can't tell how badly the Whites are dancing. If there *is* a Black at a Whites' nightclub, she's probably a Coconut and Coconuts no longer dance like Blacks for fear of appearing too Black.

Because they are so useless at modern dancing, White chicks will employ other forms of dancing. The most common alternative is called "The Twist". The Twist is a really simple dance Whites' parents invented back in the 1960s because they couldn't dance either. All you do is bend your knees, lean slightly forward and then kick your heels from side to side while making a running motion with your arms. This dance is so easy that it gives the impression that the White chicks can actually dance. At Whites' nightclubs DJs periodically play songs from the '60s or '70s to which the chicks can do the twist. This makes the White chicks feel fantastic about themselves.

How to dance like a White girl
(no talent required)

STEP 1 — Be a White Girl
STEP 2 — Bend Knees
STEP 3 — Lean Slightly Forward
STEP 4 — Make Running Motion with Arms / Kick Heals Side to Side

If White chicks can't dance then I don't know what to say about White guys – except that they are even worse than the chicks. When White guys try to dance they just end up shifting their weight from one foot to the other and allowing their arms to wobble next to them. Sometimes a White guy will bite his lower lip, clamp his eyes shut and shake his head to the music –

that's how bad White guys are at dancing. He may even clench his fists and do little punches at the same time. White guys know they are the world's worst dancers and that's why they don't hit the dance floor unless they're piss drunk and there are groups of dolled-up dancing girls.

The first thing White guys do when they get to a nightclub is go to the bar and buy a round of drinks. Then they move onto the dance floor and jostle one another to get close to the huddles of chicks. Once they're well positioned the guys try to pick up the chicks, but not with the same technique used by Black guys, where they offer their pelvises to the Black chicks for grinding. To pick up girls, a White guy taps her on the shoulder and mutters some indecipherable pick-up line into her ear. If the girl smiles and engages in conversation, the guy will try to talk to her over the extremely loud music for about one song before he's ready to have a kiss – whether she likes it or not. It's at this moment that the White guy pulls out "the Claw".

The Claw is a technique used to get a chick to kiss you even if she doesn't want to and White guys swear by it. It works like this: While his arms hang by his side, the guy flicks his right hand inwards and locks the wrist, thereby forming a makeshift claw. Shielding the Claw from her sight, the guy moves smartly towards her, pretending to whisper a sweet nothing in her ear. When he's close enough, he swiftly swings his arm around behind her and locks the Claw firmly onto the back of her head. Once locked in place, he retracts the Claw back toward himself, dragging the fighting, writhing woman ever closer to his salivating mouth. The Claw fully retracts until she's close enough for him to slobber all over her mouth. At this stage the guy waits to see if she kisses him back. If she does (believe it or not some White girls are so easy they do kiss these savages back), he releases the Claw and they spend the remainder of the night sucking on each other's faces. It's very classy. If she doesn't kiss him back he'll slobber once more on her face for good measure before releasing the Claw. That's when she slaps him and tells him to piss off. Persistent White guys will move along and try the Claw on another chick but most guys prefer to return to their buddies at the bar and attempt to drink enough so they can vomit. That's also very classy.

Going on holiday…

Because they spend so much time working hard, being ambitious and making rules, Whites need regular holidays. And they *really* love their holidays. Every year the Whites will take leave from work and spend a few weeks at a beach house, a lodge in the bush or they'll go tramping around overseas. Whites use their holidays to:

> Sleep a lot

> Lie in the sun

> Swim

> Practise their hobbies

> Train for endurance sports

> Play golf and tennis with other Whites (and the occasional Coconut)

> Read books

> Watch TV

> Stuff their faces with food, snacks and sweets

> Get piss drunk

On holiday Whites allow the stresses of real life to melt away as they spend quality time with their family and friends. The only things that get Whites a little cranky on holiday is not being able to go to the beach on New Year's Day because all the Blacks are there. And once they return home from their holidays, Whites are ready to dive straight back into their ambitious pursuits.

Affording themselves some pleasures…

White men have made an incredible contribution to society. Come to think of it, they've probably given more to South Africa (and the world) than any other demographic. They really are the true torch-bearers of everything that is good – just ask them and they'll tell you all about it. According to them, being so spectacular is not as easy or as glamorous as it looks because they have such huge demands on their time, meaning they carry a burden far greater than any other person. Thankfully for all of us they bear that burden anyway. What a great bunch. All they expect in return for their priceless contribution are two small things.

Firstly, they want to be left alone while driving. For a White man, his car is a little cocoon of peace and solitude. He prefers to drive alone with the windows up, the air conditioning on and his favourite CD playing – it's his due reward for being such an asset to society. It also gives him a chance to be alone, centre his thoughts and simply take a breather from the unrelenting demands of life as a White man. Possibly, he'll form a mental picture of himself training for an endurance event. Unfortunately for him, though, not all members of the South African public can respect this right. The most inconsiderate of these are the people who stand at traffic lights, begging and selling cheap Chinese junk. The beggars simply don't care that, by making an eating motion with their hand while standing at a White's window, they're being both bothersome and inconsiderate to the White. When beggars do this it really ticks off the White men, who try to ignore them by looking straight ahead until the traffic light changes to green, before speeding off.

Sometimes though, if you're driving with a White man and a beggar comes to his window and makes an eating motion with his hand, the White will say something to you to justify looking away. What he'll most likely say is, "I don't believe in giving money to beggars. There's no point because you're actually not helping them. You know what they say: give a man a fish and feed him for a day, but teach a man to fish and feed him for a lifetime." Despite professing this philosophy, I am yet to see a White man giving fishing lessons to a beggar at a dam or river on a Saturday afternoon. Although to be fair, I do see a fair amount of Whites taking poor-looking people with them around the golf course on the weekends. These poor-looking people are usually carrying the Whites' golf bags so I assume they're teaching them to play golf instead; because, I've heard, if you make it as a golfer you can make a lot more money than if you make it as a fisherman.

The second thing White men want is the freedom to buy Christmas presents for themselves. White men love to reward themselves for being such great guys by buying themselves Christmas presents. I have a friend who works at a bank and one of the guys he works with arrived at the office in a new Porsche Cayenne last December. My friend told him he liked his new Porsche and the guy said, "Yes, thanks. I worked hard all year so this is my Christmas present to myself." Then my friend asked him what he got his wife and he said a toaster. Now there's a silly woman if you ask me – she should've asked for something nicer.

Sometimes White guys don't have enough money to buy an ideal present for themselves *and* their girlfriends, so they attempt to kill two birds with one stone by buying for the girlfriend the present *they* wish to receive. That way they get to use it when the girlfriend isn't using it, which is pretty much all the time. Like this one guy I know: last year he went out and bought an Xbox 360, with five shoot-em-up games, and wrapped it up for his girlfriend for Christmas, even though she hates video games and violence. When she opened it up he said to her, "Oh baby an Xbox 360, just what you wanted." And she thought, "No loser, this is what *you* wanted. I wanted the box set of *Grey's Anatomy.*" But instead of telling him this – remember, White women prefer not to communicate in a straightforward manner with their boyfriends and husbands – she sarcastically said, "It's lovely." But he didn't get the sarcasm in her voice and he immediately hooked the Xbox up and spent the rest of the day playing games, while she sat on the couch bored out of her mind. Every now and then he asked her if she wanted to play and told her how stoked he was she got the Xbox for Christmas. Oh man, she was so upset that she broke up with him – she said he was too selfish for her, or something like that. You'd think he'd be bummed about it but it turns out he's not. He says he prefers playing Xbox anyway.

On illness...

Whites don't generally suffer from the same diseases as Blacks like tuberculosis, dysentery and Ebola, mainly because they don't make coal fires in their houses or drink water that has poo in it or play with monkeys from the central African jungle. On top of this, Whites usually have the means to afford private healthcare which means that even if they get tuberculosis, dysentery or Ebola they'll get some expensive medicine and be fine, whereas Blacks are often sick for years at a time. Yet that doesn't necessarily mean Whites are healthy, because they suffer from diseases that Blacks have no problems with, and which can't be cured by expensive medicine. The major disease that cripples Whites is something called anxiety. I wasn't too keen on reading a whole psychobabble book on anxiety as research for this book, so I'll just give you the short version of what the disease is about.

Anxiety is when you spend so much time worrying about stuff that you can't go through a day without spending every moment worrying. It usually results in the sufferer getting headaches and skin rashes and struggling to take deep breaths and having to go lie down for no reason.

Blacks don't struggle with anxiety at all. Like we said earlier, anytime a Black gets a little stressed or tired, he just goes and has a sleep under a tree. In fact, it's almost impossible to explain anxiety to a Black. For example, an anxious White guy is talking to his Black friend about his anxiety:

WHITE GUY: (with anxiety) "I'm sick."

BLACK GUY: (perplexed) "Really? You don't look sick and you're not coughing either."

WHITE GUY: "No, I'm not sick like that. I have anxiety."

BLACK GUY : (still perplexed) "Anxiety? What's that?"

WHITE GUY: "Well it's where you worry all the time and it makes you sick."

BLACK GUY: (even more perplexed): "Really? I didn't know worrying can make you sick."

WHITE GUY: "Well it can."

BLACK GUY: "So what does this… anxiety… do to you?"

WHITE GUY: "It makes me have headaches and skin rashes

and I struggle to take deep breaths and sometimes I just need to go lie down. I think I'm also developing a nervous twitch."

BLACK GUY: "Well, that doesn't sound *too* bad. But if it is so bad then why don't you just stop worrying?"

WHITE GUY: "I can't."

BLACK GUY: "Why not. You started worrying, so why don't you just stop?"

WHITE GUY: "Just because I can't."

BLACK GUY: "Well what do you worry about? I mean, you live in a R2-million house with electric fences in a posh neighbourhood, you drive an Audi with six air bags and ABS brakes, you have a great cushy job at a bank, you go overseas on holiday every year and you eat Woolworths organic food every day. Why are you worrying?"

WHITE GUY: "Well, I used to just worry about a couple of things, like dying or getting hurt. But then I started worrying about other stuff like getting all my errands run on time and keeping up to date with my guitar lessons and achieving all my goals before I die."

BLACK GUY: "So are you saying you worry about not having enough time to get everything done?"

WHITE GUY: "Yes, that's exactly it. I'm just too busy."

BLACK GUY: "Well why don't you switch over to Africa Time? Then you'll always have enough time to get things done. Or just do less."

WHITE GUY: (horrified) "I can't do that!"

BLACK GUY: "Why not?"

WHITE GUY: "Well because then I wouldn't be a success and people would think I lack ambition."

BLACK GUY: "Yes, but at least your anxiety would be gone."

WHITE GUY: "I know but I can't do that – it's too much to ask to convert to Africa Time. Also it is an honour to be stressed out for us Whites."

BLACK GUY: "What? You can't be serious."

WHITE GUY: "No really. Whenever I ask my friends how they are, they tell me they're *so* stressed at work and that they're *so* busy. If I can't also say that I'm also stressed and busy then I look like the guy who's not getting anywhere in life."

BLACK GUY: "Okay, just hang on a second. So you're telling me you want to *be* stressed so your White friends can give you credit for it, but you don't want to *feel* stressed?"

WHITE GUY: "Exactly. That's exactly what I'm saying."

BLACK GUY: "That's the dumbest thing I've ever heard in my entire life."

WHITE GUY: "No it's not. If you're stressed it means you're doing something meaningful with your life."

BLACK GUY: "Okay, whatever man. I don't understand you Whites, but carry on anyway. Is that all you worry about?"

WHITE GUY: "No, there's more. Then I started worrying about dust getting on the furniture and dropping crumbs on the carpet because my wife will kill me if she finds crumbs on the carpet, and not having enough money to retire. After that I started worrying about the fact that worrying was affecting my health – so I was worrying about worrying. And now... now I don't know what I worry about. I just worry all the time but I can't really tell you what I'm worried about."

BLACK GUY: "Whoa, that's pretty screwed up dude. Really, you should do what I do."

WHITE GUY: "What's that?"

BLACK GUY: "When you get a little stressed, just go lie under a tree and sleep for an hour. When you wake up you'll feel much better."

WHITE GUY: (horrified again) "I can't do that!"

BLACK GUY: "Why not?"

WHITE GUY: "Because I'm worried ants will bite me. And I'll probably miss an appointment. Also if anyone saw me they'd think I have no ambition and my reputation would be ruined."

BLACK GUY: "What? You can't be serious?"

WHITE GUY: "I'm serious."

BLACK GUY: "Okay, then I'm sorry, I can't help you. Even talking about this is tiring me out – I'm going to lie under a tree for an hour. See you later – and good luck with your anxiety."

White women can be approximately one thousand times more anxious than this.

Chapter 3:
AFRIKANERS
(White Afrikaans-speaking people)

On being world champions…

Afrikaners are the world champions… of complaining. They beat the Ukrainians into second place. If you walk past an Afrikaner talking to his friend, there is a 93 percent chance he'll be complaining.

The amazing thing is that Afrikaners actually like to complain. In fact, they love it. And complaining strangely brings meaning to their lives – a bit like Blacks and their toyi-toying. Afrikaners love complaining so much that they'll spend an hour complaining about South Africa and then end off by saying something like, "Man, I love this country so much." It's very weird.

Most people hate it when they're faced with a complainer. I once told an Afrikaner to have a positive attitude instead of complaining, and you know what he said? He said, "What's the use? A positive attitude doesn't change anything." For a statement like that I have no retort. Now it's different when two or more Afrikaners get together because they actually love to listen to complaints as much as they love to complain. When someone complains to them, it gives them new ideas and helps to jog their memory about something they wanted to complain about.

Afrikaners are so used to complaining that if they're not complaining they don't know what to say. If you ask your Afrikaner friend how he's doing he'll usually respond with an hour of complaints, but if he's got nothing to complain about he won't say he's doing fine and then talk about something happy. Instead he'll say, "I can't complain" or "I've got no complaints". Then he'll wait for something to come up that he can complain about.

The top five things Afrikaners complain about are:

1. No rain
2. The Blacks
3. Potholes
4. Land claims
5. Quotas in sports teams

On being professionals...

The reason they complain so much about the rain is because most Afrikaners are either farmers or have relatives who are farmers. This all goes back to their heritage. Afrikaners are actually a very young people – a new breed of sorts. It all started in 1652 when a boat of scurvy-mouthed Dutch sailors dropped anchor in Cape Town near the southern tip of Africa. They'd been sent by some big corporate company in the Netherlands to establish a fruit market so ships sailing between India and Europe could stock up on fresh fruit and vegetables. So the Dutch sailors planted their little veggie garden and all was fine until other people started arriving – French and British and more Dutch and Malaysians and who knows what other breeds.

The original settlers decided they didn't want to be infringed upon by these new people and they wanted their own state. They wanted freedom. So they declared themselves free citizens and threw their belongings into ox wagons, headed northeast and told everyone they were on a Great Trek. They eventually made it through the desert and mountains of the Karoo and found some nice farming land. Unfortunately for them though, they saw some half-naked Blacks running around with spears and these Blacks were living on their new-found land. This was not ideal. So the Afrikaners fired their guns and told the Blacks to *voetsek*, which is Afrikaans for go somewhere else. The Blacks put up a bit of a fight but eventually voetsekked and the Afrikaners settled into farming the land.

Afrikaners are brilliant farmers. South Africa's soil is about as fertile as a granny's uterus but these people have managed to extract every bit of goodness from it to develop a strong agricultural industry and feed the country. They grew their herds of livestock, protecting them from wild animals; they planted all sorts of grains and fruits and vegetables; and they employed sophisticated farming techniques, thereby delivering incredible yields from their land. Their wealth increased and people ate well.

There is nothing more satisfying for an Afrikaner than to walk in his lands and look at his cows grazing or watch their teats being milked, or walk in a maize field and break off a head of corn and rub the kernels in his hands. Some Afrikaners have also branched off into farming game, or wild animals. The game farmers charge hunters to shoot the animals for sport. Instead of cooking the meat like you might expect, they drench it in vinegar and salt and spices and hang it in the garage for three weeks and when it's dry enough they cut it into strips and eat it while watching rugby. This is called *biltong* and it's a lavish and tasty snack. Afrikaners sometimes wonder why Blacks don't choose to eat more biltong because it really is delicious.

Afrikaners believe there is no job more honourable than being a farmer. They are very, very proud of their farming heritage. Come to think of it, they're proud of many things. Afrikaners are very proud of the Great Trek and that they survived much adversity on their journey through the Karoo hundreds of years ago. Honestly, I don't see what all the fuss is about – I've driven that road a hundred times and I didn't find it very adverse at all. On the contrary, it is very pleasant. Furthermore, I find the idea of doing a trip through the Karoo in an ox-drawn cart quite appealing. I imagine I'd sleep under the stars every night, have delicious bacon-and-egg breakfasts in the morning and sit around a campfire in the evenings with some biltong and a glass of merlot. How splendid that would be! That's probably what it was like anyway, but you know these Afrikaners… they love to complain.

Sadly for them, today there are far fewer Afrikaners farming because those Blacks they originally told to voetsek have returned and now want their land back. Some farmers have sold their land back to the Blacks and others are still holding on. Either way, the Afrikaners complain about land claims because really, what an injustice it is to be kicked off your land.

The Afrikaners who did leave the farms have moved to the towns and cities and found other jobs. The top five jobs other than farming for Afrikaners are the following:

1. Bank manager
2. Plumber
3. Electrician
4. Glass salesman
5. Construction foreman

On selling ice cream…

Afrikaners are fairly well spread over the socioeconomic spectrum. Most of them are middle class or upper-middle class with a few who are stinking rich. Once they've made some money, stinking rich Afrikaners buy useless toys. These toys include – but are not limited to – caravans, motorcycles, ski boats and beach buggies. But the favourite useless toy of all Afrikaners is a Jet Ski.

If you're at a dam and you see a guy on a Jet Ski, wave him down. When he comes over to you, ask him if he's Afrikaans. I bet you he'll say yes. You see, the reason for this is that only stinking rich Afrikaners are irrational enough to waste R150,000 on a "water motorcycle". If you've ever ridden a Jet Ski on a dam you'll know that the fun lasts for about seven minutes, after which you're just wasting petrol racing up and down an expanse of flat water. After the first seven minutes the Afrikaners revert to zigzagging behind boats and ramping over their wakes as they go. I tried to find an Afrikaner who could explain to me why they do this, but I couldn't find any – they must all be dead (having crashed into some other boat or a jetty, I guess). Some Afrikaners who've become bored with riding their Jet Skis on a dam will venture so far as to take their Jet Skis to the ocean. This usually spells the end of the Afrikaner's relationship with Jet Skis because one of three things happens:

1. He crashes into a surfer, paralysing him for life.
2. He stalls the thing out at sea and must be rescued by the NSRI.
3. He gets dumped by a wave, and rider and Jet Ski land up crushed on the rocks.

After his first trip to the ocean the Afrikaner decides the Jet Ski is too dangerous and sells it in the junk mail for half of what he still owes on it. And then he buys a four-wheeler motorcycle and a similar process is repeated.

If you are white and not in the middle class or higher, you are a Poor White and that is not a good thing. Poor Whites are often called White Trash. Or, in Afrikaans, *Wit Rommel*. Other Whites strongly believe that being White Trash is worse than being an Indian or a Coloured or even a Black because Whites should know better. Despite being poor, White Trash do still manage to make money. Three quarters of White Trash secure jobs in the motor industry as mechanics, tow-truck drivers or panel beaters.

Occasionally a White Trash will try break away from the motor industry and he'll try to make it on his own. White Trash who break away buy ice-cream trucks because they're the only people foolish enough to believe they actually make money. Until they start driving around in the things, they believe driving an ice-cream truck is a great job, because:

> They'll enjoy the freedom of being self-employed.

> Kids love ice cream so there is always a market for your product.

> They can work flexible hours.

> They get to eat as much ice cream as they want.

> They'll make good money.

But after their first week on the job, they discover that:

> There's no air conditioning in an ice-cream truck and people only buy ice cream on the hottest days of the year. So you spend your life in stinky, sweat-drenched clothes, driving around in the sweltering heat.

> You're not allowed to play your own music from the loudspeakers. The only thing you get to play is that irritating ice-cream-truck song.

> On any given day you make R100 from selling 50 ice creams but you spend R93 on diesel so your net profit is R7 for eight hours' work.

> You eat so much ice cream you die of a combination of fatty heart disease and diabetes within three years of starting out on your exciting new business venture.

On deliciousness…

Some Afrikaners don't like to speak English. Why? Well, it all started in the late 1800s when the Afrikaners discovered gold in Johannesburg. They were very excited about their discovery and they told some Blacks to go dig it out for them. The English in Britain caught wind of the discovery and, never ones to turn down the chance to exploit another country's wealth, they went to Johannesburg and told the Afrikaners to piss off, which is English for voetsek. The Afrikaners didn't want to voetsek so they had a war.

The Afrikaners were winning the war because they hid behind rocks and bushes and shot at the columns of English soldiers that marched in broad daylight and wore lovely brightly coloured outfits. The English were also losing because they were getting very bad sunburns from the hot South African sun. They didn't take this into account when they came to fight a war in South Africa. This is why some Afrikaners call English Whites *Rooineks* (Rednecks). Another thing Afrikaners call English Whites is *Soutpiels* (Salty Penises) because they say they have one foot in South Africa and one foot in England so their penises hang in the ocean and that's why they're salty. Afrikaners consider calling someone a Soutpiel an insult, but I know an English White guy who takes it as a compliment because he says he'd have to have a pretty big penis for it to hang all the way from his crotch into the ocean.

Anyway, the British then got some hats sent over from England for the sunburn and they employed some dirty war tactics to get the Afrikaners to surrender – they took the Afrikaans women and children hostage and they burned their farms. The Afrikaners couldn't stand to see their families starving and dying in concentration camps so they stopped fighting and therefore the British won the war and earned the right to tell the Blacks to go dig the gold out for *them*. Some Afrikaners are still disgruntled about all this and that's one reason why they don't like to speak English.

To be fair though, the majority of Afrikaners have let the past go and get on very well with English Whites and they do make an effort to speak English – *effort* being the operative word, because they're not very good at it. Afrikaners speak English with an Afrikaans accent, which according to some people makes them sound a bit slow. Also, despite having seen all the Chuck Norris, Bruce Willis and Steven Seagal movies, they still make fairly elementary errors in speech. Herewith some common errors:

1. When an Afrikaner woman sees a cute baby in a pram she says shame. Why shame? Really.

2. Despite inventing the rand and using the currency their entire lives, and despite the word having no Os or Ts, some Afrikaners still pronounce the word rand as *ront*.

3. Afrikaners don't realise that a pair of jeans has two legs, hence being called *a pair of jeans*. Instead they will say something like, "This is my favourite jean pant."

4. If you ask an Afrikaner if he can speak English and he thinks he can, he'll reply that he speaks English very deliciously. This makes no sense because delicious is an adjective used to describe something that tastes good.

5. Concord is not a concept Afrikaners grasp well and that's why you'll often hear Afrikaners say things like "Those guys is my friends" or "I are wearing a jean pant". Furthermore, trying to explain it to them *are* futile, so don't bother.

6. Afrikaners can get angry sometimes which may cause them to make threats. Unfortunately their threats are often lost in translation. For example, if you make an Afrikaner angry by flicking him on the ear or something, he might bend down and pick up a stone and make the threat "I'll throw you with this stone".

You're left dumbstruck and can't help but laugh and think *where* is he going to throw the stone and me? Seriously, what kind of threat is that… throwing you with a stone? You'll generally end up laughing at him, thereby making him angrier.

7. Afrikaners struggle to place their tongues against the bottom of their top incisor teeth and blow, thus making the "TH" sound. But they're good at placing their lower lip against the bottom of their top incisors and blowing, thereby making the "F" sound. This makes it difficult to understand what they're saying. So you may hear the sentence "I'll frow you wif a stone" when you were expecting "I'll throw you with a stone". Afrikaners can also put their tongue on the roof of their mouth and make a "D" sound. In which case you may hear "I'll frow you wif da stone", if the Afrikaner in question already has a stone in his hand.

8. Finally, you should take no notice of the first two words of an Afrikaner's response when you ask him a question. His answer will always begin with the words *Ja nee* (Yes no) or *Ja no* (Yes no, if he is trying to sound more English). You can ask an Afrikaner if he wants to go to the shop with you and he will reply, "*Ja no* I will." This leaves people confused, wondering, well, what is it – yes or no? If you ignore the first two words you'll get the official answer, which is, in this case, "I will."

Even though they have been known to butcher the English language in these (and various other) ways, Afrikaners always speak English to English Whites because English Whites are even worse at speaking Afrikaans. But while English Whites think it is funny to listen to Afrikaners speak English, Afrikaners cannot bear to hear their language being desecrated by a Rooinek.

On having easy-tanning skin…

I can spot an Afrikaner from a mile away. Really I can. I could be walking down a narrow alley in a tiny mountain village in the middle of the Tibetan Himalayas and if an Afrikaner walked past me I'd know it. I used to think I had some special superpower that allowed me to spot them, but after thinking about it some more I realised that it isn't actually that difficult. You too can spot Afrikaners by paying attention to the giveaway signs.

Whether they're highly intelligent or not, Afrikaners often appear to be concentrating really hard. This look of concentration is all in the mouth really. The mouth will do one of two things. First, it may be closed really tight. The jaws will be clasped so tightly together that the lips will actually give way and be pushed out. And this will be accompanied by a constant frown. Now you may say all people can appear to be concentrating really hard. That is true. But the difference is this: most people will appear to be concentrating really hard when solving an algorithm or trying to remember if the capital of Sweden is Oslo or Copenhagen, but some Afrikaners will appear like this even when performing menial tasks like turning on the TV or tying their shoelace. Second, if the mouth isn't clasped shut, it will be slightly open with the tongue shyly poking out like a turtle's head.

Afrikaners usually have easy-tanning skin, hence the reason why they didn't get bad sunburns like the British in the war (and they also had hats). It's okay to tell an Afrikaner that he has easy-tanning skin. But never, ever imply that their skin is so because they mated with the *Strandlopers* (Beach Walkers) and *Hottentots* (Hottentots) hundreds of years ago – nothing infuriates an Afrikaner more. The Strandlopers and Hottentots were native people with light-brown skin who were living on the beach in Cape Town when the scurvy-mouthed Dutch sailors arrived. They were good at running and fishing. Some people think the Afrikaners intermingled with these darker-skinned natives and that is why their skin is so good at tanning. But like I said, don't ever mention this to an Afrikaner – he'll throw you with a stone. Anyway, the point is Afrikaners usually have easy-tanning skin.

The other noticeable characteristic of Afrikaners is that, on the whole, they are giants. If you are six foot three inches and weigh 100 kilograms, you are considered a weenie in the Afrikaner community, and if you're any smaller than that you get beaten up for it. The biggest Afrikaner I ever knew was this guy who played rugby (Afrikaners are very good at rugby) and he was in my class at university. He was two metres tall and weighed 120 kilograms and he was a chunk of pure muscle. I asked him how he got so big and strong and he said he was just born like that. He hadn't even been to gym once in his life and his biceps were bigger than my thighs.

Size of Afrikaners in relation to other Humans

Average Size Afrikaner

Average Size Human

Those are the personal characteristics I look out for when I'm spotting Afrikaners. Others include a mullet hairstyle and a scraggly beard. But honestly, the easiest way to spot one is to look at how they're dressed. It's quite simple really, as long as you remember this one important truth: Afrikaners do not follow fashion trends. Afrikaners dress the way their fathers and their grandfathers dressed. Dress sense is a tradition passed down through the generations and that is why if you look at a 20-year-old Afrikaner it's likely he's dressed the exact same way his father was dressed when *he* was 20.

Here are the distinguishing fashion accessories of an Afrikaner:

Rugby shorts

Afrikaners believe that showing off their thighs is sexy (even though this is clearly not true) so they wear the shortest shorts they can find: rugby shorts. They aren't too fussy about colours and a pair of shorts can last up to fifteen years. On that note, you can tell how old a pair of rugby shorts is by how much they're frayed on the hems and if the elastic around the waist is completely stretched. If this is the case, the shorts will reveal a plumber's crack when the Afrikaner bends over to pick up a stone and this is not very appealing. The shorts are often worn without underwear so when the Afrikaner sits on the tree stump next to a camp fire, other people may be exposed to a view of his hanging balls. This, too, is not very appealing.

Shirts

Afrikaners dress for practicality. That's why they wear these shirts called two-tone shirts, made of the toughest, thickest cotton known to man. The shirts are called two-tone because different sections of the shirt are dyed one of two colours. The colours are usually khaki and green, but they can vary. Sometimes they are khaki and brown or even khaki and blue. Another benefit of the two-tone shirt, besides being durable and comfortable, is that it helps the Afrikaner to blend into his surroundings when walking on his farm. Afrikaners like the way they look in two-tone shirts, but no-one else does and Afrikaners are the only people in the world who wear these shirts – except for White English students who sometimes wear them if they lose a bet. If the Afrikaner isn't wearing a two-tone shirt he'll be wearing a really old T-shirt he got for free at the farmer's market. The T-shirt usually has holes in it from climbing through barbed-wire fences and displays a caption like PLATRAND OESFEES 1992: GEBORG DEUR KUNSMIS KONING (Platrand Harvest Festival 1992: Sponsored by Fertilizer King).

Shoes
Afrikaners have very thick soles to their feet and therefore they like to walk barefoot, even in public places. But if they can't for some reason walk barefoot, they will only wear three types of shoes: Hi-Tec hiking boots, strops or *veldskoene* with red laces (field shoes with red laces). Veldskoene are an Afrikaner's favourite type of shoe. They are cheap, durable, made of a single flap of leather and are excellent for farming.

common Afrikaner attire

Two Tone Shirt · ←Rugby Shorts · ↑ Exposed Thigh · ←Bare Foot · ↑ Thick Sole

On fun...
Afrikaners are reserved people. They maintain composure and attempt to carry themselves in a respectable manner at all times, especially when others are watching.

Where Blacks dance and sing at every opportunity, Afrikaners only do so on special occasions, like weddings. And their dancing is orderly and formal. They do not, under any circumstances, grind. Neither do they click their fingers or wave their arms or make "woo woo woo" sounds. They never dance without a partner either. In fact, the only dancing they do is called *Langarm Sokkie* (Long Arm Socky). This entails the man and woman standing in close proximity to one another, while the man puts his right arm around the woman's waist and the woman rests her left hand on his shoulder. They hold hands with their free hands and lock the elbows so the arms are straight. The man then leads the woman in a series of shuffles, spins, twists and other elaborate dance moves as they work their way around the dance floor in a strictly anticlockwise direction.

Sometimes English Whites will try Langarm Sokkie but they won't move at the correct pace or in the strictly anticlockwise direction and the Afrikaners will purposefully bump them off the dance floor with their elbows. Afrikaners hate English Whites messing up the order on the dance floor. I know an English White who this happened to and he said he was more scared on that dance floor than when he ran with the bulls in Spain.

While they're dancing, the Afrikaner's lips will be pushed out by his clasped jaw and he'll be frowning and he'll appear to be concentrating really hard. The woman will have her head held high with her nose in the air and she'll exude an aura of sophistication. Together, they will look pompous and unhappy, but trust me: they're having the time of their lives.

When they do this dancing, there is only one type of music that's played. It's called *Sokkie Treffers* (Socky Hits) and it's the biggest-selling music genre in South Africa. Making a Sokkie Treffer CD is the easiest thing in the world:

1.   Find a singer with an Afrikaans accent.
2.   Get the backing tracks to some international hit songs.
3.   Let the singer sing the words to the backing tracks.
4.   Add some fast drum beats to give the song a more "hopping" beat.

The other thing Afrikaner men do for fun is go fishing. Boy do they love fishing. The type of fishing they enjoy is called *papgooi* (porridge throw). The Afrikaner puts a hook and sinker on his line and puts some mielie pap (yes, the food Blacks eat every day) on the hook and throws it in a dam. He then props the fishing rod up on a forked stick and that's about it. On average the Afrikaner fisherman will get one bite per day. If he's a good fisherman he can get two bites, and the pros can catch up to one fish per day.

This type of fishing is not the most active sport, so in order to pass the days between bites the Afrikaners revert to drinking their favourite drink: brandy and Coke. Brandy and Coke is more affectionately known as karate water, because it makes Afrikaners fight. If you go down to any dam in the Free State province on a Saturday morning you'll see little clusters of Afrikaner men sitting on camping chairs, shirts off, huddled around their propped-up fishing rods. Each man will be sipping from a glass of brandy and Coke as he suns his round belly. As the day wears on they'll get louder and louder as they get drunker. Then, around the time of sunset, all around the dam skirmishes will start breaking out.

It usually starts with one group of Afrikaners looking casually over at another group (Afrikaners don't like people looking at them for no reason). One of the Afrikaners being looked at will say to the onlookers, "Why you looking at me funny? Stop looking at me."

The onlooker will reply with something like, "I'll look wherever I want," to which the Afrikaner being looked at will reply, "Like hell you will, stop looking at me or I'll knock you flat." Then both sets of Afrikaners will get up and charge towards each other and start pushing and tackling and punching and trying to get each other into headlocks. This is one of only two times an Afrikaner will not carry himself respectfully. Anyway, these fights always end in one of two ways. Either both sets of guys get too tired to continue and give up simultaneously, or one of the guys gets a bite and has to run away to strike his fishing rod.

On sport...

Like Blacks, Afrikaners like only one sport. Rugby. Afrikaners are very good at playing rugby. Many Afrikaners would have you think that they invented rugby and that rugby belongs to them. (Rugby was actually invented in England but don't mention this to an Afrikaner even if he appears not to know it.)

Every Saturday Afrikaners love to watch rugby and their favourite team to watch is called the Blue Bulls. The Blue Bulls are a team from Pretoria and they are the most successful rugby team in South Africa's rugby history. A Blue Bulls rugby game is the only other time, besides when fishing, that Afrikaners will not carry themselves respectfully. On the morning of a big game, they'll get dressed in everything blue – a blue two-tone shirt and a blue jean pant or rugby short, and some of them even paint themselves blue. They'll also wear a blue helmet to which are attached some real bull's horns and some of them even wear a nose ring.

About four hours before kickoff they'll pack their cars with a bag of wood and a portable braai and their cold box filled with ice and *boerewors* (farmers sausage) and lamb chops and karate water. They'll park their car near the stadium and make a braai and drink some karate water with their friends. Then skirmishes break out, which only end because the game is starting. They all stream into the stadium and find their seats, after which they spend the entire game cheering and waving their flags when the Blue Bulls score. It's a wonderfully electric atmosphere in the stadium when they're winning; but if they're losing things can become very tense.

As soon as the Blue Bulls start losing, every Afrikaner becomes a qualified international rugby referee and will scream his interpretation of the laws at the real referee on the field. Needless to say, the referee cannot actually hear over the crowd's noise so some Afrikaners try to get his attention by throwing *naartjies* (tangerines) at him. One time an Afrikaner even ran on to the field and tackled the referee to get his attention because he'd run out of naartjies. That turned out to be a bad idea because apparently referees dislike being tackled even more than they dislike having naartjies thrown at them.

On naming their children...

Names are very important to Afrikaners and they usually follow a traditional pattern in naming their children. A child is usually named after the last three generations of fathers. That's why Afrikaners often have names like Johannes Petrus Stephanus Potgieter. Despite having these elaborate names, the guy's friends will usually just call him Piet, or JP which, if you ask me, defeats the point of having such a fancy name.

Besides shortening unnecessarily long names, Afrikaner men love to have nicknames for each other and generally these nicknames don't stray too far from their farming roots. Common nicknames include: *Klip* (Stone), *Volstruis* (Ostrich), *Baksteen* (Brick), *Os* (Ox) and so on. I once even knew a family of three brothers who were nicknamed, in descending age order *Bees* (Cow), *Kalf* (Calf) and *Kleinkalf* (Small Calf).

On the men...

Afrikaner men, as we've seen, are big and strong and manly. Despite being very masculine, they are not known for being the world's best lovers. I'm sorry, but they just aren't. People from Italy and France are passionate and sexy. Afrikaners are not. I knew this Afrikaner guy once and I asked him what his idea of the perfect romantic date was.

This is what he told me: "Da most romantic date for me are to braai some steak and boerewors while my wife make da salad and potatoes. Den we go walk in da kraal to look at da cows and afterwards we have a *koeksister* (cake sister) wif some coffee. Den we has 90 seconds of missionary-position sex and den we sleep nicely."

I guess you can't blame the men entirely for their lack of passion because Afrikaner women aren't exactly the first women you think of when you feel a burning in your loins. Argentinean women, yes. Israeli women, maybe. But Afrikaner women… nope, sorry. Afrikaner women are very sweet, respectful, loving, serving and loyal, but you don't exactly associate them with sexiness. And that's okay. I mean who says being sexy is better than being a good cook? Not me. I think Afrikaner women should stick to what they're good at. Some Afrikaner women try to be sexy but it ends up being a disaster because they inevitably go out and buy some animal-print lingerie. And no-one finds that sexy.

Afrikaner men are simple at heart and only want a few things out of life. These things include:

> A wife

> A piece of ground with some cows or springbuck

> A Toyota Hilux 4x4

> To watch rugby on a Saturday

> A couple of Blacks to clean the house and mow the lawn

On the women…

Afrikaans women, I'm afraid to say, are the least ambitious women on the planet. An Afrikaner woman only wants two things out of life:

1. A husband

2. An eye-level oven

Afrikaner women are homemakers at heart and there is nobody to match them. Their entire lives are geared to looking after their husbands and kids and they are brilliant at it. They cook, clean, scrub, bake and serve all day long. No-one will take better care of a family than an Afrikaner woman.

Now before you protest and tell me that many Afrikaner

What Afrikaner Women want

women go to university and get professional degrees and are actually very intelligent, let me fill you in on a little secret here. Afrikaner women only go to university to find a husband. I'll tell you why.

Back before the Blacks came and told the Afrikaners to voetsek off their land, all Afrikaners lived on farms. For an Afrikaner man, the way to get a wife was to go to the farm to the left and to the right and see what women were on offer. He'd then pick one for his wife (if there was more than one to choose from) and they would have children who would follow the same process. But when the Afrikaners got chased off their farms many of them moved to the cities and towns and went to school and university because they would have to get jobs other than farming. This meant there were fewer men on the farms and many of the Afrikaner women were left wondering who was going to marry them. (It was probably a good thing they went to the cities because their gene pools were already shrinking and we all know what happens when gene pools shrink: people start marrying their relatives, which is almost always not a good idea.)

There were obviously now Black men living on the farm to the left and the right of the remaining women but they weren't too keen on marrying the Blacks. So the women said, "We must go to where da men is." The men were at university and so they went to university and started studying and getting degrees.

This strategy worked well for most Afrikaner women, who secured their eye-level ovens without much delay. Sadly for some, it hasn't panned out too well. The problem is that some of these women became too educated and the Afrikaner men questioned whether they would want to be subservient wives. The Afrikaner men steered away from these women who were left to either continue studying and remain spinsters, or act dumb and pretend like they'd never studied. A lot of Afrikaner women chose the latter option.

Afrikaner women are very reserved and attempt to appear classy at all times in order to attract a husband. That's why you'll never see an Afrikaner woman with a beer in her hand, unless she's carrying it to a man who's watching rugby. Afrikaner women only drink wine – anything else just looks trashy.

Afrikaner women are quite varied in appearance. Some are pretty butch, with square jaws, the shoulders of shot-put throwers and legs that can kick-start Boeings. But not all Afrikaans women are like this. Some of them are actually totally hot. And they've learnt to doll themselves up with lots of makeup and to dress more scantily, like English girls. This has resulted in more Afrikaner girls being in demand with English guys. But honestly, whether they're butch and scary or slim and hot, all Afrikaner women end up looking the same. When they hit 35 they immediately double in size, cut their hair short and dye it maroon or purple, and they switch to wearing loose-fitting pants and floral blouses with shoulder pads.

On women's hobbies...

Once they get married all the stress of life melts away and Afrikaner women settle into the same routine they'll follow until the day they die. They cook, bake and clean for their husbands, manage the maid and gardener, shop for groceries and pursue their hobbies. Boy do Afrikaner women love their hobbies. The top ten hobbies of Afrikaner women are:

1. Knitting
2. Crocheting
3. Folding laundry
4. Baking desserts like milk tarts and koeksisters
5. Cooking roasts
6. *Skinnering* (talking about their friends behind their backs)
7. Making potpourri
8. Shopping for antiques
9. Making flower arrangements for the NG Kerk bazaar
10. Making jam

Of the ten, their favourite hobby in the whole world is making jam. Every Afrikaner woman has a jam recipe that's been passed down through four generations. Inevitably, at some stage she will plant her own plum or apricot trees and she will unearth her great-grandmother's recipe for jam and make some for her husband's toast. And in a particularly good year, she'll make enough jam that she can give some to her neighbours as presents. Afrikaner women, more than anything, are proud of their home-made jam.

Chapter 4:
INDIANS

On coming to South Africa…

There are a ton of Indians in South Africa and if you talk to one he'll tell you that the Indians in Durban are very different from the Indians in Port Elizabeth who are very different from the Indians in Cape Town who are very different from the Indians in Pretoria – and so on. Don't worry about all that. All you have to know is there are generally two types of Indians in South Africa: Indian Indians and South African Indians.

Indian Indians have recently migrated to South Africa from India or are here on work contracts with multinational companies. South African Indians are also originally from India, but they've been in South Africa for 150 years. A whole bunch of them were shipped to South Africa in the second half of the 19th century as indentured workers for the sugar plantations in Natal, but that gig didn't last too long. Most of them were released because they were virtually useless on the plantations, and if you've seen an Indian's body you'll know why. Indians have no muscles. None whatsoever. Even the strongest

Indian cannot lift more than an eight-year-old Afrikaner boy. The man who paid money to ship out those original Indian workers must've lost a fortune on them because Indians just aren't built for back-breaking manual labour like chopping down trees and carrying bundles of sugar cane. My friend is a White and he works at a bank and there are tons of Indians working there and he says almost all of them have hunched backs – even the force of gravity is too strong for them.

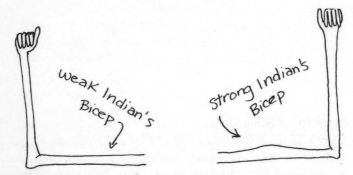

Indian Biceps

Weak Indian's Bicep

Strong Indian's Bicep

It's a mystery why Indians have such underdeveloped muscle tone. My friend at the bank suspects they don't get enough nourishment because of all the fasting they do. He says the Indians at work are always fasting because of some or other holiday, which makes no sense to him and other Whites. Whites do the exact opposite on their holidays – they prefer to stuff their faces with as much snacks, food, desserts and drinks as they can lay their hands on and then they lie on the couch for the rest of the day. And if you ask most Whites if they fast, they laugh and tell you yes they do, from breakfast until lunch.

Because of this lack of muscle tone and the tendency to go for long periods without eating, you generally won't find Indians succeeding at any one of the following professions:

> Body builder
> Golf caddy
> Boxer
> Food critic
> Sugar-plantation slave

On becoming westernised…

In some respects, South African Indians have retained much of their original Indian roots and traditions. For one, they all still look and sound like Indians. Second, their favourite food is still curry. And third, they love to watch Bollywood movies.

In the whole world there are only two types of people who watch Bollywood movies: Indians, and Whites who want to appear culturally diverse. For everyone else, watching a Bollywood movie arouses the same agony as when a woman scratches her nails down a blackboard. This is due to a combination of hammy acting, cheesy dialogue and constant scene interruptions by random and uncalled-for synchronised singing and dancing. These interruptions are the worst part of Bollywood movies. If you've never seen one then let me explain.

A perfectly good scene will start with a handsome young man talking to his beautiful girlfriend at a dinner table in a restaurant. (The movie is a love story, by the way, because Bollywood *only* makes love stories.) He declares his undying love for her and, starry-eyed, they both lean in for a passionate kiss. The girl is usually pretty hot and you've waited about two hours to see some action, so you're on the edge of your seat. And then, as their lips are about to touch, something completely unexpected happens – the lovers and the other 80 patrons in the restaurant all spring from their chairs and break into a choreographed song and dance. I mean really, when has that ever happened in real life? It starts to get on your nerves after a while.

In other respects though, South African Indians have become more westernised. For example, South African Indians will ask for a "cooldrink in a glass", instead of a "mineral in a tumbler", which is what an Indian Indian usually asks for. However, the most significant way in which South African Indians have been influenced by Western culture is their acceptance of the sit-down toilet.

Last year my friend went to India to get in touch with her spiritual side and when she came back she told me, among other things, that most people there use Eastern-style toilets (also known as squat toilets) and they don't use toilet paper either. Instead they scoop water from a bucket with their hand and splash it onto the underside of their bums.

That news fascinated me because I know some South African Indians and the majority of them don't bother with the Eastern-style toilets any more – they've become accustomed to the sit-down option. I must be fair, though, and say there are exceptions. Some Indians still swear by them. I have an Indian friend and he is a real die-hard Indian: he goes to India every two years and his wife always wears a sari and they're always burning incense in their house. He converted all his sit-down toilets to the Eastern-style version because he says he likes to uphold the traditions of his ancestors, and he actually prefers them from a practical perspective. Now I think that's just wonderful; not only because I love ancient traditions, but I must be honest and say I'm a big fan of the Eastern-style toilet.

Firstly, it's a whole lot easier to relieve yourself (my doctor told me the squat position straightens out all the twists and turns in your colon so the lamb vindaloo you ate the night before doesn't have to do so much navigating in order to get out). And secondly, I'll have you know that I find the whole water-splashing technique surprisingly refreshing.

I would even support a motion to convert some public toilets in South Africa to the Eastern-style version. Maybe then there wouldn't be such terrible queues outside the loos at busy events. One time I had to wait for twenty minutes at a restaurant because some White guy was trying to finish the last chapter of *The Da Vinci Code* while sitting on the loo. White guys love to read while on the loo, but really, some people can be so inconsiderate. If that had been a squat toilet, I bet that guy wouldn't have been in there for longer than a minute because most people can only squat for about 45 seconds before they get a charley horse in their leg. So like I said, I'm a big fan.

But not everyone is as positive as I am about this squatting business. Some people are totally allergic to the idea. I have this one White friend who refuses to squat. He's a lawyer and he drives a Volvo and he only stays in 4- or 5-star hotels when he goes on holiday, and overall he thinks he's much fancier than he actually is. One time we went on a hiking trip and he refused to do a poo for four days because he said squatting is barbaric and he'd rather wait until he gets home. He spent the entire last day of the hike wincing every time he took a step. Amazing, hey? I always figured one of the joys of camping was you had a loo everywhere you looked.

Anyway, the point is that most Indians in South Africa don't use Eastern-style toilets any more, but others still swear by them.

Eastern Style Toilets vs Bush Toilets

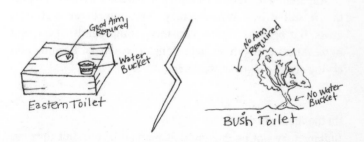

Spotting the difference...

Indians are pretty easy to spot. They have brown skin and thick dark hair and they smell like curry spices. Now, Indians' skin colour varies from light brown to dark brown and every shade in between, but this is not representative of how much time they spend lying in the sun – they're just born that way. Amazingly, some Indians are so dark that they're even darker than Blacks, but this does not make them Black because they don't have above-average-sized lips or very curly hair.

Telling the difference between Indian Indians and South African Indians can be trickier than telling the difference between Indians and Blacks, or Indians and Whites. This is because both Indian Indians and South African Indians look like Indians. The only noticeable differences are that Indian Indians like to wear very bushy moustaches and they snort a lot in public and will spit just about anywhere. South African Indians don't really spit much in public.

Whether they're from India or South Africa, it might be a little risky to shake hands with an Indian. That's because all Indians give limp handshakes that feel like you're grabbing hold of a dead fish, and it feels a bit gross. My White friend who works at the bank hates it so much that he doesn't shake hands with Indians any more – he just gives them knuckles. He also gives knuckles to all Blacks because he says Blacks consider you one of the brothers if you give them knuckles.

Apparently for Indians a limp handshake is a sign of respect but it still drives Whites crazy. Not only because it feels gross, but because Whites consider a limp handshake a sign of weakness and Whites hate signs of weakness. Begging and crying are also signs of weakness.

On the theory of sales...

Indians may not be any good at manual labour, but they are seriously good at selling stuff. Back in the 18th and 19th centuries Indians mostly sold things from India, like spices and fabrics and other Indians. But today Indians will sell anything they can get their hands on, from fishing rods and computers to leather shoes and sardines (more on that later). But I'll tell you what – they're the best at selling you stuff you don't want.

When Blacks try to sell you stuff, they tell you their family will die if you don't buy their product. When Whites try to sell you stuff, they tell you *your* family will die if you don't buy their product. Indians use a completely different technique and it's called Indian giving. It works like this.

If a White walks past an Indian's shop in the middle of a thunderstorm and he's getting soaked, the Indian shopkeeper will run outside and shove an umbrella in his hand and say, "Hey boss, you look like you're getting wet. Here, have this umbrella."

The White says thanks and as he walks away, the Indian says, "Hey boss, where are you going with that umbrella?"

And the White says, "What do you mean? You gave it to me."

And the Indian says, "No my larney, I didn't give it to you for free. You must buy it if you want to take it."

And the White says, "No way, I'm not paying for it. Here take it back."

And the Indian says, "Sorry, but I can't take it back. You've used it and I can't sell a second-hand umbrella."

And the White says, "Well how much is it?"

And the Indian says, "R100."

And the White says, "Are you bloody mad? I'm not paying a hundred rand for a stinking umbrella! That's daylight bloody robbery, man!"

And the Indian says, "Okay I'll give you a special price. Half price, but only for you and only today." (This is the second leg of the Indian selling technique – making someone believe that they are giving them, and only them, and only today, a very special price.)

And the White, thinking it's not too bad to have an umbrella to keep him dry in this storm and thinking it isn't too bad to get an umbrella for half price, pays him the R50.

The White goes on his way, happy he's dry and got a good deal on an umbrella. And the Indian chuckles to himself as he slips the money into his back pocket, because inside his store the umbrellas are selling for R40.

Besides selling stuff, Indians are excellent at being:

> Call-centre consultants

> Accountants

> Bankers

> Pharmacists

> Doctors

But if they're not one of those things it's most likely the Indian is an IT guy. Indians love to be IT guys and they're masters at it. Whenever a person has a problem with their computer and they call the IT department, the Indian will appear at their desk and will have the problem fixed in no time. Solving the problem usually involves downloading some upgraded software off the internet and uninstalling a hidden application and then reconfiguring the computer's mainframe... or something along those lines. The Indians always know what to do.

My friend at the bank says he's so relieved when an Indian shows up to fix his computer because the problem always gets sorted out. His only complaint is that it gets a little irritating when, after the problem is resolved, the Indian always says something like, "I sell flash drives on the side. You interested? I'll give you a special price. Only today though."

One of the other reasons why Indians so often choose to be IT guys is that they gain access to the passwords for the network firewalls, which means they get to download music, movies, ring tones and pictures of naked women (if they're so inclined) without having to pay for the bandwidth. If you do the calculations this benefit adds up to a substantial cash saving each month.

On proximity to sardines...

Indians can be spotted all over the country but the overwhelming majority are still lingering in the province of KwaZulu-Natal, and more specifically within a hundred-kilometre radius of Durban. There are three reasons for this:

1. Durban has the largest Indian community.

2. Durban has the best curry.

3. Durban's weather is most similar to India's (hot as hell).

Despite that, the number-one reason why Indians stay close to Durban is to take part in the annual sardine run. Each year, between May and July, millions of sardines swim in shoals up to twenty kilometres long along the East Coast, past Durban. The fish are rounded up and attacked by sharks, dolphins and an array of game fish, such as shad, kingfish and tuna. It's a feeding frenzy – for the fish and the Indians alike. Indians love fishing as much as Afrikaners, except they prefer fishing in the ocean to papgooi. When taking part in the sardine run they employ one of two fishing methods.

Method one is to run into the ocean with nets fabricated from bed sheets and patio awnings to catch as many fish as possible and drag them out onto the beach, while doing their best to avoid the snapping jaws of the sharks.

Method two is to stand on the piers and beaches with fishing rods, attempting to hook a game fish. Believe it or not, standing on the beach or a pier during the sardine run is even more dangerous than being in the water with the sharks. The Indians stand shoulder to shoulder and three rows deep holding their twelve-foot long fishing rods like lances, rigged with sinkers the size of cannonballs and hooks that resemble rappelling hooks. They wait in anticipation, like a nervous, besieged army. As soon as the Indians spot the big dark mass of fish approaching, the frenzy begins. Someone shouts "Tight lines!" and the next thing every Indian simultaneously swings his fishing rod behind his back and hurls his tackle at the approaching swathe of sardines and other fish in the ocean.

It's total carnage out there – thousands upon thousands of Indians get injured. The top four injuries and causes are:

1. Concussion – anglers suffer concussions due to being struck on the head by the cannonball-sized sinkers hurtling through the air.

2. Hooks in eyes, ears, noses and arms – anglers in the rear generally get hooked by the front men as they're casting, often ripping open their flesh.

3. Hooks impaled in feet – anglers inevitably drop their tackle boxes and hundreds of hooks end up in the sand, like little landmines.

4. Black eyes – skirmishes naturally break out in the chaos as men fight to untangle lines and jostle for the best positions along the pier or beach. Black eyes result from punches to the face. Thankfully, nothing worse than a black eye results from these punches because no Indian is strong enough to inflict a more serious injury.

Indian after Sardine Run

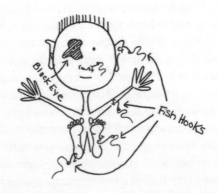

On cookouts...

If you see a group of fifty-plus Indians, don't assume it's a religious or political gathering. Chances are it's a family outing. Indians have very large families and they love to get out of the house on weekends and public holidays. Their favourite thing to do on these days is take the whole family, including senile and otherwise bed-ridden grandparents, on a family picnic to a dam, a river or the grass embankment at the beach. The main purpose of these outings is for the men to play a cricket match while the women cook a curry from scratch. Despite being in close proximity to water, the purpose of these outings is not to swim, so swimming costumes are seldom taken along. In fact, Indian people are scared of being exposed to too much sunlight because they'd rather not become any more tanned than they already are. This is called the Snow White Complex and it's the reason why you'll never see an Indian in a swimming costume or shorts while outside in the day, and why they always play sport in jeans. But after playing sport in jeans, the Indian men get very hot and they usually end up wanting to have a quick dip after all, so they just swim with all their clothes on. Most Whites don't understand this behaviour.

Because the families are so large the men are able to pick two full cricket teams. Wickets are pegged in the ground and batsmen pad up and put on helmets because they prefer to play with a real full-sized Kookaburra cricket ball rather than a (seemingly more sensible) tennis ball. So you'll have three or even four generations of Indians playing an entire 50-over cricket match. It's amazing to watch because they are masterful with a bat or at bowling spin. In recent years though, Indian families have switched to playing 20-over matches to mimic their latest obsession, the Indian Premier League (IPL). The games are shorter and more explosive because they get to hit more sixes and fours. And some Indians even let off fireworks at the dam, river or beach when their team-mate hits a six.

The problem with this type of exciting, six-hitting, fireworks-exploding cricket compared to the real IPL, is that there are usually Whites lying on the beach next to where the Indians are playing. These Whites don't appreciate being hit in the chest with a real full-sized Kookaburra cricket ball while sunning themselves. After being hit in the chest, the Whites will usually consider keeping the ball before they throw it back begrudgingly and mutter under their breath why don't these Indians go somewhere else. (Whites hate mobs of people disturbing their peace.)

While the men are playing cricket the women off-load industrial-sized pots and pans, plastic bags of food ingredients, cases of two-litre Cokes and portable gas stoves, and they get to cooking a chicken curry from scratch. The curry usually cooks for three hours – the duration of the cricket game. Once the game is over everyone sits on the grass to eat the meal and discuss the cricket match. Usually the Indians will stick around until long after sunset, lazing around, eating more curry, kicking around a soccer ball and drinking Coke. By that stage the Whites have all left because Whites know that beaches, dams and rivers are not safe after sunset. The only thing that gets the Indians to go home is to watch their favourite soccer team play on TV. Indians only support four soccer teams: Manchester United, Liverpool, Arsenal or Chelsea. If you don't know which one of these teams is their favourite, just take a look in their car where you'll see either an official Manchester United (or other) banner or scarf on the backboard, or a team sticker covering the entire back window.

On the women...

Indian women love shiny things. Their favourite shiny thing is yellow gold because it contrasts so well with their brown skin. I tell you what, yellow gold really does look very good on Indian women. And they know it – they sure do enjoy acquiring elaborate necklaces, rings and bracelets for themselves. Other shiny things they love are press studs, fake gemstones and those silver half-moon things that look like fish scales which they stick on their clothes.

Indian women also love colours. They have many favourite colours depending on the context. As we've discussed already, their favourite colour for jewellery is gold. For clothing, their favourite colours are red, yellow, sea-blue and bottle-green because that's the colour of most of their saris. And as for houses, their favourite colours are pink and turquoise. If you drive through an Indian neighbourhood you'll see evidence of this.

Indian women can be super hot (sexy-hot, that is, not curry-hot) when they're young. But they can't seem to carry that beauty through into middle and old age because there aren't too many slim-and-sexy middle-aged Indian ladies around. It seems that literally overnight they put on 30 kilograms and their skin gets splotchy and they wear more traditional Indian clothes like flowing robe-like saris, instead of the tight-fitting skirts and low-neck tops they wore when they were young. From this moment on they're called Aunties by all in the family. And they can be so immature – I mean really, some of them stick these little red dots on their foreheads between their eyes. If you haven't seen one they look a bit like the blue felt tips you stick on the end of a pool cue, except they're red. Supposedly the red dot means the woman is married, but I think that's kind of immature because I quit sticking things on my forehead when I got to grade two. (Before that we would get a gold star to stick on our heads if we got all our sums correct.) Also they like to draw squiggly lines all over each other's hands when they get married. That's another thing I quit doing when I was in school – drawing on other people's hands.

But while they're young, boy do Indian girls get the guys' engines revving. Indian guys are forever smelling their perfume and ogling their slim bodies and dolled-up faces and long, dark hair. Even White guys, both English and Afrikaans, have started to take notice of the Indian girls (now that it's legal) and most Whites would love to have an Indian girlfriend for a while. Just for a while though… to see what it's like. My White friend at the bank really thinks Indian girls are gorgeous, but he says there's one thing he can't deal with. Their sideburns. For some reason Indian girls have hairlines that drop right down to the level of their earlobes and their sideburns are precariously close to being classified as lamb chops. The problem my friend has with that, besides that women are not meant to have facial hair, is he says he likes to suck on girls' cheeks (it's just something he does) and he's not too keen on getting a mouthful of hair when he does that. I don't blame him.

On the men…

There is only one thing Indian men like more than Manchester United, Liverpool, Arsenal and Chelsea. Cars. Indian men are obsessed with cars. No matter his financial position, an Indian man will always have a souped-up car. And if he's rich, an Indian man will buy himself a really nice car – and then soup it up some more. The top six favourite cars of Indian men are:

1. VW Golf GTi
2. Mercedes C-Class Coupé
3. Audi S3
4. BMW M3
5. Subaru Impreza WRX STi with gold mag wheels
6. Any red car (because red cars are faster than cars of other colours)

Indians who can't afford to buy expensive cars will count their money and determine how much they have to spend on a car. Let's assume it's R45,000. They'll take that figure, and divide it into three. A third, R15,000, is to buy a car. The car is usually a Toyota Corolla RSi, a VW Citi Golf or an Opel Kadett GSi with at least 200,000 kilometres on the clock. Another third is to soup the car up with aesthetic and performance accessories. These accessories include, but are not limited to:

Performance Accessories	Aesthetic Accessories
Free-flow exhaust	Rear spoiler with built-in additional brake light
17-inch low-profile Michelin tyres	TSW mag wheels
Jetted Mikuni carburettor	Tinted windows
K&N high-performance air filter	Custom-made oversized bumper kit
Eibach performance suspension springs system	Wood steering wheel and gear knob
NOS (Nitrous Oxide System)	Metallic pedals

Chances are you'll probably *hear* an Indian's car before you see it. What you'll hear is either the boot spoiler vibrating or the same rave song playing over and over. This is because the final third of the money is spent on a sound system. The sound system will usually consist of a BOSE, Pioneer or Alpine front-loader CD player and six or eight interior speakers. Usually it isn't necessary to look in the car to find out what brand the sound system is because a sticker bearing the sound system's make will take up the entire width of the windscreen or rear window (quite often accompanied by a Manchester United, Liverpool, Arsenal or Chelsea sticker). Note that if you ever drive anywhere with an Indian be sure to pack light because all the boot space will be taken up by an external amplifier and a 12-inch sub woofer. The average Indian man is so proud of the sound system in his car that he hangs a CD from his rear-view mirror.

Besides pointlessly driving around town so people can see and hear them, the other main use Indians have for their cars is to transport them to casinos and horse-racing tracks where they gamble the night away.

When they're not gambling, betting or selling stuff, Indian men will either be found hanging around in pool halls or trying to pick up blonde White chicks in nightclubs. Indians go nuts for blonde White chicks. Unfortunately for them, their fancy cars and gelled hair often aren't enough to lure a White chick. White chicks generally don't go for Indian guys because they like men with muscles (although muscles won't necessarily guarantee you a White girlfriend if you are a White who has red hair or if you are a Black). Some Indian men have resorted to going to gym and drinking protein shakes and creatine to get some muscles in order to get a White chick. And some of them do succeed, but at some stage the White chick will see the Indian man with shorts on and she'll notice that his calves are actually skinnier than his forearms. So she will break up with him because that just looks silly. Unfortunately there is nothing you can do about skinny calves. This is another reason why Indian men like to play sport in jeans.

Chapter 5:
COLOUREDS

On who they are…

Coloureds in South Africa are people of mixed race and, like the Afrikaners, they're also a relatively new breed. If you're unsure if a person is a Coloured or not, simply get hold of their family tree, and if any of their ancestors married someone who looked nothing like they did, then you can be sure they're a Coloured.

Coloured people originated in Cape Town where you had the native Strandlopers and Hottentots, the European immigrants and slaves from across the globe falling in love with one another. Because of their mixed-race heritage, Coloureds vary in skin tone, but more often than not they have light-brown skin. Their skin is generally lighter than Blacks' skin and only marginally darker than some Afrikaners'. (Remember, try not to remind Afrikaners about this.) They usually have curly or frizzy hair that looks like it's been crimped, but it's not often as curly as Blacks' hair.

On names...

Coloureds love to be creative with language. Some words, for example, can have completely opposing meanings depending on the context. The best example of this is the Afrikaans word *voetsek*, which is very often used by Coloureds. It is most commonly used to tell a dog, or a human, to piss off. But sometimes a Coloured woman will say it to her boyfriend to thank him if he tells her she's beautiful. In this case she'll say, "*Ag voetsek!*" but in more of a playful tone than when telling a dog to piss off. She'll also flicker her eyelashes so it's important to take note of her tone and the movement of her eyelashes to determine if she's thanking him or telling him to take a hike.

For some reason Coloureds have taken the word stupid, which is an adjective, and they've turned it into a noun. When witnessing a shouting match between Coloureds in a public place you might hear one Coloured call the other "a stew-pit" (translation: a stupid). And you'll be left asking yourself, "A stupid what? A stupid idiot? A stupid chop?" But no, the insult is complete – it's just "a stupid".

Coloureds also like to get creative when naming their children. The precedents they follow in choosing names for their children are:

1. To use names that emphasise a rolling R, like Roscoe, Kieren (pronounced Keeeeeeeren), Jerome, Roland, Warren and Brandon.

2. To use names that haven't been used by anyone else in half a century, like Basil, Meryl, Gerald, Solly, Percy and Sheryl.

3. To use names with a Middle Eastern ring to them, like Faizel, Gamida, Shaheen and Rashad.

4. To take two names and turn them into one name. For example: Wayne and Dillon makes Waylon, Elliot and Roy makes Elroy, Mike and Ronald makes Myron, and Gerald and Sherwin makes Gershwin.

On being sensitive about nothing…

Coloureds should be commended for not being overly sensitive about much at all. Some people are sensitive about *everything* – you literally can't say or do anything without their feelings getting hurt. And I'll tell you what, it's people like that who really suck the life right out of you, because you're forever having to watch what you say and do and then it's always a whole ordeal trying to cheer them up after you've (apparently!) done something wrong.

Like this one White guy I know gets really upset if he doesn't receive an invite to come out for a beer on a Friday night. He'll send SMSes at 7am on a Saturday morning which say stuff like "I hope you enjoyed your night out. I didn't" or "How many beers did you drink last night? I didn't drink any". Seriously, this isn't a joke – there are actually people in the world who do this kind of thing and they're more common than you think. And then you have to apologise repeatedly and practically buy the guy a box of muffins to get him to give you a smile. That guy really sucks the life right out of me.

Now Coloureds, on the other hand, don't suck the life right out of you because, like I say, they aren't sensitive about much at all. For example, Coloureds aren't sensitive about being called Coloureds. If you go to a place like America people are so sensitive that you can't call a Coloured a Coloured even if he is a Coloured. Some Blacks in America even refuse to be called Blacks. Can you believe that? You could walk past a Black guy and say, "Hey Black guy, nice shoes," and he'll totally ignore your compliment just because he doesn't want to be called Black. He'll only take notice if you say, "Hey African-American guy, nice shoes." It's a real pain, if you ask me. But anyway, thankfully the Coloureds in South Africa haven't further complicated our lives by refusing to be called Coloureds.

Besides not being sensitive about much at all, Coloureds also aren't embarrassed by things that turn most other people red with shame – like disciplining their children in grocery stores.

Coloureds couldn't be bothered how many people are watching while they're screaming at their children or hitting them on the back with a rolled-up newspaper; if the child needs some bloody discipline then he's going to get it. Some Coloureds have even been known to chase their screaming children around grocery stores with broomsticks they've grabbed from the shelves.

This form of public discipline is in stark contrast to the way Whites do it. Whites also realise the importance of disciplining their children, but they try to hide the process from strangers. Whites try to discipline their children as discretely as possible so as not to disrupt the shopping experience of other shoppers or give them the impression that they have unruly children and are substandard parents. That's why instead of running after the screaming child with a spatula or a mop, the White parent adopts the conspicuously inconspicuous approach.

If a White kid steals a chocolate off the shelf and stuffs it in his mouth and then sees his mother glaring at him, he'll immediately know it's time for a showdown. The kid will turn quickly and break into a brisk getaway walk toward the nearest exit or group of bystanders. The mother, too, will break into a brisk walk in pursuit of the child. Once she catches up with him (thanks to her longer strides), she'll pull up alongside him so they're walking shoulder to shoulder. The mother is now in position to administer a hiding. As discreetly as possible, she'll raise her straightened arm behind her back and swing it in a vertical arc, landing it on the child's bum. You'll know this has happened when the child lurches forward, pelvis first, followed by the rest of his body as he tries to get his bum out the way. The mother will again lengthen her stride to catch up with the child so she can get alongside him and smack him again. The entire time she'll also be scolding him out of a tiny hole she's created in the side of her mouth while looking around to make sure no-one is watching. Even though her words are not in any way decipherable, the child gets the message through the furious tone of her grunts and the swinging arm that propels his entire body forward every few steps. The most bizarre thing is that after this ordeal the mother will feel bad and buy the child a chocolate and continue shopping as if nothing happened.

Coloureds have a completely different approach. They don't try to hide anything when they discipline their kids.

One time I went to a grocery store in Cape Town and I walked past a Coloured family standing at the Coca-Cola fridge. It was a father, a mother and their son, who looked about ten years old. The son tugged on his father's shirt and said in a whiny voice, "Derrie, derrie, ken I hev a Coke?" ("Derrie" means "Daddy" in Coloured-speak. Many Coloureds have strange accents that take a while to work out.)

The father looked down at him irately and immediately ceded authority. "Naai men," he said, "don't ask me for thet. Go ask your blerrie mammy." (A "blerrie mammy" is a mother in Coloured-speak. Don't worry, you'll get the hang of it.)

I watched as the ten-year-old son defiantly took an ice-cold Coke from the fridge and cracked it open without asking his mother's permission. The mother turned to see her son drinking the Coke and this is what transpired:

MOTHER: (in a shrill voice): "Herrrold! What the hell you doing? Who said you ken hev a Coke?"

SON: (hurt and defensive) "Mammy, Derrie said I ken hev one."

MOTHER: (turning to her husband) "What?! Talbot, why the hell d'you say the kid ken hev thet kak men?"

FATHER: (raising his voice) "Naai men, I didden give him no kak. I tol' him to ask you. Dohn come kak me out here when I done nutting wrong!"

MOTHER: (raising *her* voice) "Well then discipline the

blerrie child men! He can't be drinking thet blerrie shyit all the time. His teeth is gonna rot off his face!"

FATHER: "Hey men, don't blerrie swear in front of the kid."

Meanwhile, the ten-year-old son, Harold, is happily slurping his Coke, unperturbed by the scene unfolding before him.

MOTHER: (shouting at the top of her voice): "Ja, well then you mus' discipline 'im, Talbot!"

FATHER: (now also shouting at the top of *his* voice): "Jissie, you always on my blerrie case men."

MOTHER: "Ja, it's because you a kak father. Do something you blerrie stew-pit!"

FATHER: "Ag, fok it men. Herrrold, gimme thet blerrie Coke."

MOTHER: (rhetorically): "Hey, en now who's swearing in front of the kid?!"

FATHER: (glares at his wife before snatching the Coke from his son and seeing that it's almost empty): "Jissie men Herrrold, you awready drenk the whole blerrie thing. Jissie, I'm gonna moer you when we get home! Come on, we going home now!"

MOTHER: "Herrrold, you see what kak you causing now. Come on we going!"

And just like that, the parents left their half-full shopping trolley right there and stormed out of the shop, dragging the child with them by the arm. And what's the craziest thing of all? The Whites who witnessed the drama were more embarrassed than they were.

Besides disciplining their kids in public, the top five things that turn other people red with shame but don't bother Coloureds at all, are:

1.	Smiling without any front teeth
2.	Loitering
3.	Punching, kicking and slapping each other
4.	Making a scene in public
5.	Swearing at each other in the middle of a crowd

On kissing and making up…

Coloureds can be spotted all over the country, but mostly they live in the Western Cape, in and around Cape Town. Coloureds live in Cape Town for a variety of reasons: it is such a beautiful city, the summers are splendid and that's where they originally came from. However, the number one reason they remain in the Western Cape is because that's grape-and-wine country. Coloureds really love their grapes and wine and if you drive through the Cape winelands you'll often see them in the vineyards, munching on grapes or enjoying a bottle of vintage merlot beside the road. As much as all Coloureds love their wine, nobody loves wine more than a Bergie.

Many people write off Bergies as vagrant beggars who do nothing but get drunk all the time. Well I disagree entirely – I think Bergies are remarkable people. I like to think of them as Coloureds who've elected to break away from the demands and stresses of modern society to live a life of simplicity. Everything about their lives is centred on simplicity and I think they may be onto something here, because seriously, modern life really can be quite stressful. For example:

>	Instead of going through the hassle of signing countless documents to buy a house, Bergies prefer to make their beds on the cool concrete of city pavements where they're in close proximity to shops; or in the soft,

refreshing grass of spacious meadows where they can enjoy the sights and sounds of nature.

> Instead of wasting four minutes a day brushing their teeth (not to mention having to carry a toothbrush and toothpaste with them everywhere), they just knock their teeth out – it's so much easier.

> Instead of selling out to the capitalist corporate machine, Bergies choose to make an honest living cleaning up city streets by shuttling cardboard in shopping trolleys to recycling centres.

> And instead of buying their wine in bottles and having to fiddle around with corkscrews when they're thirsty, Bergies just buy their wine in five-litre foil bags. These foil bags are called *papsaks* (soft bags) and they're an excellent innovation for Bergies and others in pursuit of the simple life. Papsaks require no corkscrew so they're easier to open and drink from. Also, when you're finished drinking your wine, the papsak can be filled with air and used as a pillow on which to lay your head, which is something you'll probably need if you've just drunk five litres of wine. And – get this – the papsaks, if filled with helium and attached to a piece of string, can also be converted into those shiny birthday balloons they sell in overpriced gift shops.

Alternative Uses for Papsaks

① Drinking Wine ② Sleeping off Hangover ③ Birthday Balloons

When they're not shuttling cardboard or drinking papsak or making birthday balloons with the empty bags, Bergies spend their time either relaxing in the sun or practising karate. I'm not sure why they practise karate because I can't really see how it fits into their simple life philosophy. Maybe it's to keep fit or something. Either way, they must be pretty good at it because I'm always seeing Bergies practising their kicks and punches on one another on pavements and in open fields.

It must be a different style of karate to the one I practised at school, though, because I never fought a Bergie at a karate tournament. *We* did the JKA-style karate and we used to wear these starched-white karate suits, but Bergies just do karate in their everyday gear. Also in our style we had to make a "Key-yah!" sound when we threw a punch or a kick, but the Bergies don't make a "Key-yah!" sound when they do so. I've heard them. Instead they make this other sound, which sounds like "Yo-mar-sip-oes". I tried to Google it but Google couldn't help me find out what karate style uses that sound when throwing kick-and-punch combinations. Sometimes they also make another sound, which sounds like "Yo-four-kin-nigh", but I couldn't find that on Google either. Looks like not *everything's* on the internet then, is it? Oh well, whatever… I guess this is just another example of Coloureds being creative with language.

On extreme makeovers…

In America and England they have lots of these shows where they take ugly-looking people and give them a makeover to help them look better. Experts are hired to fix their hair, nails, faces and dress sense and at the end of the show they reveal the new person to an audience. The audience goes berserk because they realise the person was actually not that ugly-looking – they just needed to get cleaned up a bit. The shows have been such a huge hit that they've branched into doing makeovers on people's houses and cars as well.

My friend lives in Cape Town and he produces reality TV shows and he says he has a great idea for a new South African show. It would be called "Extreme Makeover: Coloured Edition". He says he thinks the show will be a big hit because Coloured guys are the worst-dressed people in our solar system. He says you could pretty much pull any Coloured guy out of his car on any given day and you'd have the perfect candidate for a makeover. He says that if you take the average Coloured guy, there are five areas that would need to be worked on to fix up his general appearance:

1. Hair. Just cutting all of his hair the same length and having it all the same, natural colour would be a massive improvement. My friend would make him get rid of the Mohawks, spiky hair with frosted tips and/or the designs etched with a clipper into the sides of their heads, including any lines, blocks and lightning bolts (that he would no doubt have).

2. Teeth. My friend would send him to a dentist to insert tooth implants where there are gaps. Also he would remove the gold teeth and replace them with white ones.

3. Dress sense. All silk boxer shorts would have to be worn *underneath* a pair of normal shorts, and not *as* shorts. My friend thinks there are way too many Coloureds walking around in public places wearing nothing but silk boxer shorts and flip flops. Also, he would make them burn the white, orange and turquoise linen suits they so often wear, because those suits were in fashion for about one month in 1976 before they were all pulled from the shelves and dumped in landfill. That's how the Coloureds got hold of them and they've been wearing them ever since. Also, no more wearing those collared shirts that are a certain dark colour like black or blue but the cuffs and collars are white.

4.   Shoes. My friend would ban him from wearing white shoes unless he was playing sport.

5.   Eyes. My friend would definitely get rid of the contact lenses that make Coloureds' eyes look green or yellow or cat-like – Coloureds are the only people who still wear those things and they are just way too creepy. Some Coloureds do naturally have green eyes, which is also very creepy, and in their case they should wear contacts that make their eyes look brown.

My friend says he can pretty much dress the Coloured in anything other than what he usually wears and he'll look infinitely better. He thinks the show will be a hit, and I wouldn't bet against him.

On car shopping...

Just like the Indians, Coloureds like fixer-uppers when buying a car. They love nothing better than buying an old beat-up Toyota Sprinter or Golf II GTi and spraying it a different colour themselves and souping it up with performance and aesthetic accessories. When buying a second-hand car they usually look for many of the same things that Indians look for – like 16 or more valves, lots of exhaust noise and enough boot space to fit a sizeable sub woofer.

But Coloureds also look for one other attribute, which for them is the most important feature when buying a second-hand car. Does the seat recline all the way to 180 degrees? Coloureds prefer to lie down when driving, although they're not actually sleeping. Often you have to make a double take when a Coloured drives past you because you can't see anyone in the car; unless you look through the rear side window and see the very top of his forehead sticking above the level of the door. If you wonder if the person driving past you is a Coloured and you can't see in the rear side window (because it's so heavily tinted) you may want to look for further telltale signs:

> The car is sprayed pink, lime green or luminous blue and it looks like it was sprayed at home with spray cans purchased at a stationery shop.
> The rear wheels are larger than the front wheels.
> The standard lights have been replaced with LED lights.
> There is a limp arm dangling at a perpendicular angle to the road from the driver's window.

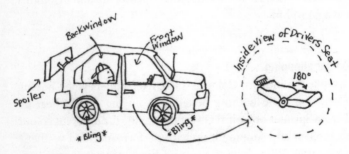

Driving 'Coloured style'

On the community of clowns...

As badly as they dress on any given day, once a year Coloureds are allowed, and actually encouraged, to wear the most hideously striking clothes they can find. At the Coon Carnival.

The Coon Carnival is the most splendid parade in South Africa and it makes its way through the streets of Cape Town every summer. In recent years people have taken offence to calling the event the Coon Carnival because they say the word Coon is defamatory toward Coloureds. (Of course, it wasn't actually the Coloureds who were offended.) So now some people call it the Cape Town Minstrel Carnival.

Around New Year's Day each year (when all the Blacks are at the beach), thousands of Coloureds from all over Cape Town get dressed in shiny, brightly coloured suits and hats and they paint their faces and they carry umbrellas and they march through the streets of Cape Town in their neighbourhood troupes, playing banjos and banging on drums and dancing and jigging about and singing songs about the months of the year. It is a wonderfully jovial affair and quite a spectacle. Some people have even said it's as good as the Rio Carnival in Brazil, but I wouldn't go that far. My friend went to the Rio Carnival and he said that there you have the added spectacle of seeing sexy Brazilian women jigging about with nothing but a layer of body paint covering their boobs. I've never seen *that* at the Coon Carnival. Although I have seen a Bergie woman getting dressed behind a tree, but that doesn't exactly compare. Nonetheless, the Coon Carnival is one of Cape Town's finest traditions and such a wonderful celebration of South Africa's cultural diversity.

Despite it being such a grand exhibition, most Whites stay the hell away from the Coon Carnival because they are scared of getting caught up in an uncontrollable mob and subsequently being mugged or stabbed. This is because, in general, Whites are terrified of Coloureds because they think they all belong to gangs and carry knives or, at the very least, screwdrivers. Also, when Whites see groups of Coloureds dancing and singing, they're not quite sure if they're having fun or if they're disgruntled and rioting. (Coloureds, like Blacks, also like to sing and dance and smile when they're disgruntled.)

Now I must be honest and say that I also stay the hell away from the Coon Carnival, but it's not because I'm scared of Coloureds – I actually find them quite agreeable. The reason I don't go to the Coon Carnival is because there are two things that scare me more than anything else in the world, and one of them is clowns. Nothing gives me the shivers more than a clown. I don't know why but those silly clothes and oversized shoes and the painted faces just terrify the crap out of me. Maybe it was because I watched that movie *It* when I was a kid.

The Coloureds who take part in the Coon Carnival paint their faces so they look like clowns to me and they wear silly clothes and hats. Being surrounded by thousands of people who look like clowns is my worst nightmare. Really, if I wasn't terrified of clowns, I'd be at the Coon Carnival every year.

Just for the record, the other thing that terrifies me is flushing aeroplane toilets. You go into those toilets and do what you've got to do and that's no problem at all. But then you have to push the little blue flush button and the next thing there's this incredibly diabolical sucking sound, and before you know it you feel like you're caught in a vacuum and you wonder if everything in the toilet is going to get sucked in and shot out somewhere over the Atlantic. That's also pretty scary.

On searching for identity...

For some obscure reason some Coloureds have come to believe that gangsters are cool. My friend joined the South African Navy in Saldanha Bay and he said that on the first day they arrived at the base there was this Coloured guy who was dressed like a gangster and he talked like one too. He had this baseball cap pulled over his eyes so he could hardly see where he was walking and he had all these ridiculous rings on his fingers. The funny thing though, was that he came from a well-to-do neighbourhood in Cape Town and was actually not a gangster – he was just trying to act like one.

Unfortunately for him, his gangster persona backfired (something he maybe should've expected in the Navy) because before they even had a chance to change clothes the Drill Sergeant made them run ten kilometres in whatever they were wearing. The Coloured guy was wearing jeans that hung under his bum, and because they were four sizes too big for him they kept sliding down and tripping him. Also, his lace-less basketball shoes were sliding off the whole time. He ended up coming in last and he got a thousand push-ups as punishment.

Then, the first time they went to the shooting range he lifted his arm above his head, turned the pistol sideways and started shooting like Antonio Banderas in a scene from that movie *Desperado*. Needless to say he sprayed bullets all over the show, endangering everyone and everything in the vicinity except the target. He got another thousand push-ups for that effort. And then – get this – he suggested drive-by shootings should be instituted as an official offensive urban-warfare tactic. Yep, you guessed it: another thousand push-ups.

On fishing...

Where Afrikaners and Indians fish for the sport, Coloureds fish to eat. Sadly for them, it's becoming harder to catch enough fish to survive because South Africa's coastline has been raped and plundered by filthy foreign fishing trawlers that don't care that they're stealing our fish, destroying our coast and making life difficult for our Coloureds. But that's a whole separate issue which we're not going into now.

Coloureds love to eat fish so much because for many generations it has been plentiful along the Cape coast. For Coloureds there is nothing better than their favourite fish, *snoek*, on the braai – they have the same affinity for snoek as Blacks have for rotisserie chicken. Coloureds also love fish so much because it is the best food to eat if you have no teeth – the soft flesh is easily chewed with nothing more than the gums.

The best place to have a snoekbraai is right there on the beach where you catch the fish. That way the Coloureds can scrape off the scales and throw the guts onto the sand to be gathered by a seagull, a stray dog or a White's unsuspecting foot. The snoek is so fresh and delicious and the Coloureds are masters at preparing it with lemon juice and butter and spices and special ingredients. It is eaten straight off the griddle, hot and sizzling, and then followed up with a squirt of wine into your mouth from a papsak. How delicious! Besides a squirt from the papsak, the favourite accompaniment to the snoek is a box of *slap* chips (floppy French fries), covered in salt and drenched in vinegar. That whole meal is one of the best you'll ever eat. Boy, those Coloureds sure know how to live the good life.

Chapter 6:
MISCELLANEOUS

South Africa is also full of minority groups – bunches of people who've immigrated to South Africa because they like it better than where they come from. These people include, but are not limited to, Greeks and Portuguese, Dutch and Germans, Chinese, and Jews. And then we have the Expatriates – people who left South Africa because they thought they'd like another country better, but they're actually still South African even if sometimes they don't like to admit it.

GREEKS AND PORTUGUESE

On supermarkets…
South Africa has a sizeable Greek and Portuguese community. You may have noticed this if you've ever bought your groceries at a Spar, where there are generally three generations of dark-

haired, olive-skinned people fretting behind the tills and re-packing the shelves and reading a newspaper in the cigarette kiosk. If they don't own their own Spar, the Greeks and Portuguese will most likely own a corner café, a coffee shop or a fruit-and-vegetable shop.

On spotting the difference…

I don't know about you, but for the life of me I can't tell the difference between a Greek and a Portuguese because Greece and Portugal are virtually the same country up in Europe on the Mediterranean (I think). If you lined up an array of Greeks and Portuguese before me, I sure wouldn't be able to separate them into their countries of ancestry. Unless I got to hear them say their names. This is because Greeks usually have ridiculously long surnames consisting of a disproportionate number of Os, Us, Ls, Ps and Ss. I bet if you just took those letters and splashed them on a page like a Jackson Pollock painting, you'd get a Greek surname. Greek surnames commonly sound like: Demopoulous, Papadopoulos and Sotiropoulos.

Portuguese surnames are also easy to identify, but in a totally different way. When Portuguese people pronounce their surnames it sounds like they've been drinking alcohol all day and they've got too much spit sloshing around in their mouths. It actually sounds pretty gross, but it definitely helps to figure out their heritage. Common Portuguese surnames are: Figueira, Mascarenhas and Vasconcelos.

Most Greeks would fiercely disagree with the notion that they look anything like the Portuguese. Greeks generally consider themselves the offspring of intellectuals, philosophers and the godly-looking, and therefore they think they're quite fancy. The Portuguese, on the other hand, are better known for being descendents of less flattering sea-faring folk. Greeks will tell you they can spot the difference, but seriously, who are they trying to kid? Greeks and Portuguese look identical! They both have olive skin that is good for tanning, and they always have really dark hair. And the guys are all as hairy as werewolves with hair growing in places it ordinarily shouldn't – like smack bang between their eyes and all over their backs and shoulders. One time my friend went to the beach and he stumbled upon a Greek family and he said he thought he'd stepped into a scene from that movie *Gorillas In The Mist* – he said he'd never seen such a hairy bunch in his life. And I'll tell you what: the women aren't far behind in the hairy department. I know this Portuguese family and all the women have so much hair on their upper lips that when you see them from afar it looks like they've all been drinking from a jug of chocolate milk. That reminds me of a joke my friend told me: Why did the Portuguese boy want to grow a moustache? So he could look like his mom. Hahaha! The point is you could tell that joke about Greeks too.

Anyway, I think we can all forgive them for their overzealous hair follicles because Greeks did introduce us to the wonders of baklava, souvlaki and Greek salad, while the Portuguese gave us prego rolls and peri-peri chicken – just as long as I don't get any hair in my food, please.

Greeks and Their overzealous Hair Follicles

Greek Grandmother — Moustache

Greek Mother — Moustache

Greek Daughter — Moustache

DUTCH AND GERMANS

On not being Afrikaners...
As previously noted, the early Dutch settlers who came to South Africa became Afrikaners. Since then, Dutch and German people have consistently filtered into the country and settled here. These later immigrants have generally succeeded in keeping themselves from becoming Afrikaners, holding on to much of their own traditions. The Dutch still drink lots of coffee and eat too much liquorice and cheese, and the Germans still drink lots of beer and eat pigs in every conceivable form.

On saving their money...
Overall the Dutch and the Germans are very agreeable people, except that they wear socks with sandals in public places, which upsets many people.

The only other irritating thing about the Dutch is that they won't let five cents go without a fight. Together with the Scottish, the Dutch are the stingiest people on the planet, no matter how rich they are. Even the Dutch who've moved to South Africa are as tight with their money as they've always been. You'll often hear Dutch people saying things like "A penny saved is a penny earned" and "Money doesn't grow on trees" and "I have deep pockets and short arms". I'll tell you what, if you're a waiter and you get a Dutch person as a customer, don't even bother giving him good service.

My friend at the bank once went to France and some French people told him they hate the Dutch (granted, the French hate everybody) because when the Dutch go on holiday to France they don't spend a cent there. Before leaving home, the clog-stompers buy everything they need for their four-week holiday at their local shops, where it's cheaper. They then pack it all into their caravan, hitch the caravan to the car, fill the car with enough petrol to get to France and back, and off they go to somewhere beautiful like St Raphaël or Biarritz or Bordeaux. They park their caravan in a camp ground and sit there for a month, enjoying their Dutch cheese and coffee, not spending a cent, and then off they go back home. I think it's ingenious. But it drives the French bonkers.

Length of Dutch man's Arms in relation to Pockets full of Money

Can't Reach Money

Meanwhile, some Germans who've recently made bucket-loads of money in a very short time move to Cape Town because it's cheaper than being in prison in Germany.

CHINESE

On saving the rhinos…
Chinese people have been living in South Africa for many generations now. Go into any small town in the country and there will be a Chinese general store that sells plastic enema kits and fireworks and all sorts of weird and wonderful

products. They really have made South Africa home – so much so that the Ministry of BEE or some such department declared recently that Chinese people can now consider themselves to be black. But this makes no sense at all because everyone knows that Chinese people are not black. Come to think of it, the only thing that's really black on a Chinaman is his hair, which is always cut in exactly the same style as every other Chinaman. (When it comes to fashion, Chinese men aren't very fashionable.) Other identifying traits of the Chinese are that they have narrow eyes, they make a cracking sweet-and-sour chicken and, even though most of them haven't returned to China since they left and they don't have any family ties in China any more, they still speak English with a Chinese accent, which means they swap their Rs and Ls and say things like "Herro, prease!" when they mean "Hello, please!"

Now that China seems to have stopped driving tanks into public squares and their doors are open to the rest of the world, it's quite likely that immigration to South Africa will increase. But look, we're not going to go on about that because, honestly, all you ever hear these days is China this and China that and it's getting really old. Everybody's going on about economic growth in China and how they're buying up the whole of Africa and how they're going to take over the world, and with 1.3 billion of them what chance do the rhinos have? It seems like people are pretty scared of China becoming the world's next superpower because there's just no telling how far they'll go to further their own interests. And then what will be left for the rest of us?

Portrait of the world's next superpower

On the silver lining...

If China *does* take over the world everyone will have to adapt and learn to deal with the negatives. For example, there will be a lot more people snorting and spitting in public and launching nasal projectiles at other people's feet. But there are bound to be positive effects as well and that's what we should focus on. The top six positive effects of China's world domination will be:

1. Finding a Chinese restaurant will be much easier because almost all Chinese families own a Chinese restaurant.

2. Increasing your movie collection will become much cheaper and easier because, incredibly, the Chinese are able to produce DVDs at a fraction of the regular cost. (The Chinese are very clever.)

3. Japanese companies like Toyota, Sony and Canon will have to cut prices on their overpriced goods as they come under pressure from authentic Chinese companies like Tayoto, Zony and Cannan.

4. As the Chinese become wealthier they will no longer want to look the same as all the other Chinese. This will create many more jobs for hairstylists who can come up with creative and differentiating hairstyles.

5. As more Chinese people interact with the English-speaking world they'll require English lessons, thereby creating many new jobs for English teachers and professors. The curriculum will include teaching Chinese people not to mix up their Rs and Ls and also not to unnecessarily add As into their sentences. The sentence, "Hello please! I'm Chinese and I speak very good English" will *not* sound like "Herro prease! I'm a-Chinese and I a-speak a-velly good Engrish."

6. Chinese people are generally pretty short and if they're going to become part of the global community, they're going to have to do something about their height. I

think there's only one guy from the whole of China who's not short, and he's *really* tall. His name is Yao Ming and he lives in America now because he's good at basketball and he is 2.29 metres tall. I have no idea how he got to be so tall – maybe he was developed in a laboratory or something – because he is about double the height of any other Chinese person. Anyway, I'm pretty sure the pharmaceutical industry will boom with sales of growth hormones for Chinese people wishing to grow taller.

But the biggest advantage of having China take over the world is that we will never have to stand in queues ever again. Boy, do I hate standing in queues! It's such a waste of time. Chinese people don't believe in wasting time standing in queues. That's why if you're waiting to use an ATM the Chinese people will never wait in line. Rather, as soon as the ATM becomes available, they'll all charge it as if they heard a starter gun go off. They'll push and jostle and force their shoulders in front of other people's shoulders and dig their elbows into each others' ribs and pretty soon everyone is standing in a giant cluster around the ATM, with those in the front having their heads squeezed against the screen. Some people think this kind of behaviour is rude and unfriendly, but I'm not too bothered – I'll do anything so I don't have to stand in queues any longer.

On South African greetings…
In South Africa a "china" is another word for a "dude". So if you say "Howzit my china" it's the same as saying "Howzit dude." But if you say "Howzit my china" to a Chinese person that's incredibly funny because it's a pun. You should do this as often as possible because Chinese people love it.

Jews

On being undercover…

Most people don't know this, but the boats that arrived in Cape Town in 1652 with those scurvy-mouthed Dutch sailors weren't only carrying Dutch sailors. They were also carrying Jews. Only they weren't allowed to call themselves Jews because the Dutch government had restrictions on the immigration of non-Christians. And even when they got to South Africa they weren't allowed religious freedom either, so for many years thereafter they continued acting as if they weren't Jews. Only in 1804 did a politician named Jacob Abraham de Mist (some people suspected he was a Jew) allow the Jews to be Jews by granting religious freedom to all people.

On requiring no discipline…

Where Coloureds and Whites employ opposing methods to discipline their children in public places, Jews have a completely different approach: let the kid do whatever the hell he wants. When doing *their* grocery shopping, Jewish parents won't be the least bit bothered while their kids run around making a racket and breaking things and irritating people and stuffing chocolates in their mouths. The parents just go about their business and they don't find this behaviour at all obnoxious, partly because they behaved the same way when they were children.

My friend is a Jew and he got away with murder when he was a kid. He was allowed to drink as many milkshakes and Cokes as he wanted and he ate sweets and chocolates and cakes until he passed out from the sugar overload. If he felt like eating pancakes for dinner or expensive Gino Ginelli ice cream for breakfast then that's what he got. He had enough fireworks in his room to start a war and he owned all the coolest toys, like Teenage Mutant Ninja Turtle action figurines, and his grandmother was always slipping money into his pocket when she saw him. He had it all, and every kid in the neighbourhood wanted his life. But now he weighs 140 kilograms and has type-II diabetes and he never stops sweating. All the neighbourhood kids now understand why their parents always said "You'll thank me for this one day" when they made them eat their vegetables. Oh well, besides being fat and sweaty and having one foot in the grave, he's actually a really nice person even though he never got any discipline.

On blowing things out of proportion...

Today there are about 70,000 Jews in South Africa but it sure feels like there are a lot more than that. Jews really seem to pop up everywhere you go – like investment banks, treasuries, golf clubs, fancy shopping centres and horse-racing tracks – and they're pretty easy to spot because they usually have dark hair like Greeks or Portuguese and they have big noses shaped like eagles' beaks. And they can really be anal about some things.

My friend at the bank says there's this Jewish guy at work and he wears this little hat but it's so small it doesn't even shield the sun from his face. My friend is bald and one day they were sitting in the sun at a corporate team building and my friend's head was getting sunburnt. He asked the Jewish guy if he could borrow his hat and the Jewish guy said no. So my friend just grabbed it as a joke and put it over his bald spot. Well, that Jewish guy lost it with him; he snatched it back and started shouting at him and telling him he can't wear his hat (he actually called it another name but my friend can't remember the word). Then my friend told him to chill out. Well that made him even angrier (don't ever tell an angry person to chill out – it just exacerbates the situation) and he stormed off and now he avoids eye contact with my friend when they pass in the corridor. I think the Jewish guy is blowing things way out of proportion because the least you can do is lend a bald guy your hat if his head is getting sunburnt.

Jewish Sun Protection

The other strange thing about some Jews is that they refuse to eat those double-bacon-and-cheese hamburgers from Wimpy. Now that's ridiculous – that's the *best* hamburger on the planet! Lettuce, tomato, relish and pickles with two beef patties, melted cheese on top and a couple of strips of fatty bacon. Just thinking about it makes me want to go get one.

One time my friends and I we were driving from Durban to Johannesburg with a Jewish guy in the car and we stopped to get a hamburger at the Wimpy. The waitress came to take our order while the Jewish guy was in the bathroom. We didn't want to wait so we ordered him a double-bacon-and-cheese hamburger because it's the best burger on the menu. But when he got back he told us he doesn't eat bacon or cheeseburgers. We almost fell off our chairs when we heard that. Have you ever heard something so ridiculous in your life? I mean really, who doesn't eat cheeseburgers? Or bacon? Bacon is like the most delicious food ever – if I could afford it I'd eat a pack of bacon every day. We tried to convince this guy to just try it but he refused. He ended up ordering a plain Wimpy burger, which is *so* boring. But whatever, that was his loss – I ended up eating two double-bacon-and-cheese hamburgers and they were delicious. Man, I love bacon.

On still blowing things out of proportion...

Then there was the time I went to a braai and there were a ton of Jews there and only a handful of Whites and Blacks and Indians. I was really dying for some pork bangers but as soon as I was about to slap them on the griddle, one of the Jews grabbed my hand and asked me not to braai my pork bangers on the same griddle as his lamb. I asked him why and he said he doesn't eat pork bangers and then I went at it again – who the hell doesn't eat pork bangers?

Anyway, just to keep the peace I went to the kitchen and fried my pork bangers on the stove, which turned out to be a good thing because it meant I got away from the conversation around the braai. Those Jews did nothing but talk about the stock market the whole night and it was driving me crazy. Come to think of it, whenever I go to a braai the Jews do nothing but talk about the stock market. It really bores me to death because I hate talking shop after hours.

No matter what their profession, every Jew is an expert on business and the stock market. It seems like they're always talking about the PE ratio of this company and dividend yield of that company and how they're planning to hedge their dollar exposure with a cross-currency interest-rate swap and how they just made a stack of money on some or other credit derivative. It sure does sound like they know what they're talking about, but I just think it's not very considerate if that's the *only* thing you talk about. I usually try to change the subject to sport or chicks but some Jew always brings the conversation back to the stock market.

When the Jews are discussing the stock market, most English White guys will try to act like they know as much about the stock market as the Jews. The Whites do this in the hope that the Jews will give them some tips on which shares to buy. The Whites will usually try to enter the conversation by relaying to the Jews the day's headline on the front page of the *Business Day* newspaper. They'll say something like "So, I see Sasol's earnings are up" and wait for a response, or they'll ask a question like "What do you think about MTN's proposed takeover?"

But the Jews aren't fooled by the Whites' false motives. This is because the Jews have already discussed this news in depth… the previous day. Either way, even if the Whites had something valuable to contribute, I don't think the Jews like to share their tips with them.

In fairness, even though it bores me to death, I guess talking about the stock market all the time pays off for the Jews because most of them have got to be pretty rich. And that's probably why they can afford to feed their kids expensive Gino Ginelli ice cream for breakfast.

There is one thing worse than talking about the stock market though: being subjected to what Jewish women talk about. They do nothing but talk about their friends behind their backs in their most nasal voices – what this one did and what that one said and who that one is dating and she can do so much better and if only she could see what a womaniser he is and what so-and-so wore to David's Bar Mitzvah and wasn't it just so shameful to her family and where did she buy those hideous shoes and can't that woman take a hint and get some dress sense.

EXPATRIATES

On similarities with Afrikaners...

Like the Afrikaners, all South Africans do their fair share of complaining about everything from the condition of the roads to quotas in sports teams. They might not do it as openly, intensely or often as Afrikaners, but on an absolute scale they sure do a hell of a lot of complaining. South Africans have even pioneered the production of TV shows that do nothing but complain. Their three favourite complaining TV shows are:

1. *Carte Blanche*

2. *3rd Degree*

3. *Special Assignment*

The purpose of these shows is to reveal to viewers everything that is wrong, sad, depressing, gruesome and soul-destroying with the country, the human race and the world. Believe it or not, South Africans like to watch these shows because it gives them a chance to voice their opinions and disgust directly at the TV. South Africans prefer to voice their opinions at a TV because a TV can't disagree with them (South Africans hate people disagreeing with them). Some parents also like to plonk their children on the couch and make them watch the particularly disturbing content to scare them into being more ambitious so that they don't end up being the victim (or the perpetrator) of such atrocities.

For example, some South Africans might be watching a report on how a fraudster embezzled millions of rands from innocent women and children. The parents will turn to their child every few minutes and say, "Do you see that? These are the kinds of people who are out there. Thieves. And they're everywhere. You have to watch out because *anyone* can be a victim. And you see that guy over there, the crook? That's what you'll land up like if you don't get straight As at school or make friends with the rich kids. Just you remember that."

Some South Africans, after watching too many episodes of complaining shows, decide that it would be better to live in another country where everything is perfect. Mostly, these are English Whites and Afrikaners, but Blacks, Indians and Coloureds have also been known to do this. After thinking about it for about 11 seconds they decide to go where South Africans go to die: Australia. Unfortunately for them, most South Africans who decide to move to Australia never actually make it there, because getting into Australia is almost impossible. Australia is ridiculously advanced and First World and unless you're highly educated and have three degrees or you have millions of rands in the bank, you're considered a passenger, and Australia doesn't take passengers.

Once they discover that they can't get into Australia, they will move swiftly to plan B, which is to emigrate to New Zealand. I like to think of New Zealand as Australia's rehab centre for people who aren't yet fit to be Aussies. It's much easier to get into New Zealand because New Zealand is just… not great. But once you've been there for three years you get a passport which allows you to work and live in Australia. Sadly for them, many South Africans don't get out of rehab and never realise their goal of making it to Australia to die.

Those who do eventually make it to Australia will settle mostly in Sydney, Melbourne, Brisbane and Perth. And – quite astonishingly – many of them find that Australia is not in fact the utopia they were hoping for. It's just another place with its own set of problems to complain about. So inevitably they start complaining again, except about completely different things than when they lived in South Africa. The top ten things South Africans complain about in Australia are:

1. Not being able to break the speed limit or drive drunk

2. Not being able to make a wood fire in your garden

3. Too many rules

4. The cost of housing

5. The flies

6. The Australian accent

7. The Australians

8. Too many Asians and Greeks

9. Missing *Carte Blanche*

10. "As great as it is, it's just not South Africa"

I knew this one Afrikaner guy who moved to Perth and he hated it. I asked him why he didn't move to Sydney or Brisbane and he said he wanted to be in Perth because it was closest to South Africa. That really cracked me up – I laughed and told him he had one foot in South Africa and one foot in Australia and that makes him a Soutpiel. Boy, was that a bad idea! That guy lost it with me! He was furious and he started defending himself, telling me this was completely different to the English Soutpiels, but I couldn't really see the difference. He doesn't talk to me any more, but whatever, if he can't handle the truth then that's not my problem.

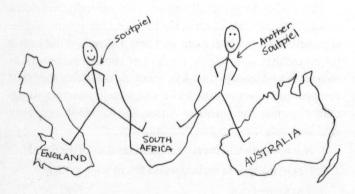

South African Soutpiels

On the other option…

I must be fair though and say not all the South Africans who move to Australia hate it. Many settle in to a happy and safe life away from the problems in South Africa and they have a great life in their new home, and they even start talking with an Australian accent. But enough about Australia. Another place to which South Africans relocate is England. More specifically, London. There are tons of South Africans in London, mostly young people, working and threatening to travel Europe in their spare time. These are temporary expats.

The most splendid thing about relocating to London and becoming a temporary expat is that by simply being in London the South African is doing something great with his life. For parents, having a child in London allows them to answer proudly when their friends ask them "So what's little Jimmy doing with his life?" (English Whites especially love to ask after other people's children so they can work out whose kids are better.) The parents will be able to respond proudly, "Oh Jimmy, he's in London." This will impress the other parents and they won't feel the need to ask any more questions like "What's he doing in London?" and "Where's he living in London?" which is a good thing considering Jimmy is working as an internal mailman in a bank (even though he has an honours degree in Finance) and he shares a three-bedroom, one bathroom house with twelve other people and he gets piss drunk and eats Texa Fried Chicken every night.

Besides threatening to travel extensively in Europe, South Africans go to London to experience the "culture" and make money. Just before they move to London, they will email their buddies who are already there (every South African has buddies in London) and ask them what they earn and what they pay for food and rent and travel expenses. After gathering the information, they'll do a quick calculation which will look something like this:

Sadly for them, their aspirations of achieving financial freedom don't quite materialise. The actual budget ends up looking more like this:

Travel card	(£40)
Rent (a room in a house shared with 12 other people)	(£100)
Entertainment (can only afford to spend £20 a week on a few beers)	(£20)
Total:	£240
Money saved each week:	£80
104 weeks, less 6 weeks for trips back to SA, and less 2 weeks for being off sick from eating fast-food burgers made with British mad cow beef = 96 weeks	
96 weeks x 80	£7,680
Converted to rands at 11:1 (pound has weakened against the rand)	R84,480
Less unforeseen costs not budgeted for:	
Plane tickets back to SA for holidays and all your friends' weddings	R30,000
Cold and wet weather clothing not necessary in SA but indispensable in London	R5,000
Psychologist consultations to help you get over the depression of not seeing sunshine for two years	R10,000
Rehab costs because you've become an alcoholic because there is nothing to do in London but go to the pub	R15,000
Total saved in 2 years	**R24,480**

Conclusion: not as enticing as first thought.

Needless to say, South Africans in London love to complain as much as their counterparts in Australia. The top six things South Africans in London complain about are:

1. No-one talks to each other on the tube.
2. Black dust in your nose from the tube.
3. Sweating on the tube on the way to work because you're surrounded by people, and then spending the whole day at work smelly.
4. It's always cloudy and raining.
5. Having to look at British people's teeth all the time.
6. Having to clean your own house.

Like the Afrikaner guy who moved to Perth, most South Africans living in London are Soutpiels because they desperately miss South Africa and are always wondering whether they should move back, even though that would mean they no longer get to come back to South Africa and proudly buy drinks for all their friends because, in their own words, "It's okay, I'm earning pounds."

That's why while they're in London Soutpiels try as much as possible to keep in touch with their South African roots. They do this in the following ways:

1. Living with South Africans in and around Wimbledon

2. Braaiing no matter the weather

3. Only going out to South African pubs like Springbok's and Zulu's

4. Skyping their parents every other day

5. Buying Ouma Rusks, Mrs Ball's Chutney, Marmite, boerewors and biltong from their local South African shop at eleven times the price it is in South Africa

Anyway, if I were them I'd just move back to South Africa. Then they wouldn't have to be Soutpiels and miss South Africa so much. And honestly, paying R500 for a kilogram of biltong is more than I could handle. But hey, who asked me, right?